ABIDE

"With the wisdom and vulnerability that only a truly humble and healed guide can have, Heather Khym will lead you into the heart of God and usher in a reawakening of your own heart. The practical tools and stories shared will give you the language and courage to engage your own story. And the best part is, you don't have to do it alone. Khym's words gently extend the Savior's healing hands to you on every page. This book will help you to go deeper, be healed, become more free, and fall deeply in love with Jesus and the life he's crafted for you. I wholeheartedly recommend this book to anyone at any stage of their spiritual journey."

Beth Davis
Director of Ministry Advancement
Blessed Is She

"By recounting her own arresting and very personal journey, Heather Khym provides a pathway to healing the interior wounds that afflict all of us. She wants us to engage our relationship with the Lord as our life truly is—not as we wish it was or as we pretend it to be. With gentle humor and practical tips, Khym guides the reader to engage the 'abundant life' that Jesus promises to those who trust in him."

Most Rev. J. Michael Miller, CSB
Archbishop of Vancouver

"If you feel alone, wonder if things will ever change, or are longing to experience the abundant life that Christ promises, then *Abide* was written for you. Soul healing is not reserved for the precious pious or the holy huddle; it's an offer to each one of us, and Heather Khym is an unparalleled guide on that journey. She shares her story, and in doing so, accompanies you as you explore your own. Dive into these pages and engage with the wisdom found here and I promise you, you will be changed for the better."

Lisa Brenninkmeyer
Founder of Walking with Purpose

"*Abide* is a gold mine of wisdom about the challenges of life, emotional healing, and spiritual transformation. In sharing about her own experiences of healing, Khym leads us to the very heart of Jesus. Her touching personal stories are mixed with sound and practical theological reflections showing us the way to live in truth and love. If you long for deeper intimacy with Jesus, you will love this book."

Bob Schuchts
Author of *Be Healed*

"If you have been longing for a friend to walk with you through the fragile places of your life and to where your heart aches for restoration, this book is for you. With delicacy, truth, wisdom, and beauty, Heather Khym invites you into the heart of Jesus and into the abiding love of the God who never leaves you nor forsakes you. This practical and inspiring book will bring healing to your life and will bless you immensely."

Sr. Miriam James Heidland, SOLT
Author of *Loved As I Am*

"I appreciate how Heather Khym is practical in her approach, instilling confidence that a new life in Christ is actually possible."
From the foreword by **Fr. Dave Pivonka, TOR**
President of Franciscan University of Steubenville

ABIDE

A Pathway

to Transformative

Healing and Intimacy

WITH JESUS

HEATHER KHYM

AVE MARIA PRESS AVE Notre Dame, Indiana

Nihil Obstat:
Most Reverend J. Michael Miller, CSB
Archbishop of Vancouver

Imprimatur:
Most Reverend J. Michael Miller, CSB
Archbishop of Vancouver
August 12, 2021

The *Nihil Obstat* and *Imprimatur* are official declarations that a book or pamphlet is free of doctrinal or moral error. No implication is contained therein that those who have granted the *Nihil Obstat* or *Imprimatur* agree with the contents, opinions or statements expressed.

Foreword © 2022 by Dave Pivonka, TOR

Founded in 1865, Ave Maria Press is a ministry of the United States Province of Holy Cross.

www.avemariapress.com

Paperback: ISBN-13 978-1-64680-117-6

E-book: ISBN-13 978-1-64680-118-3

Cover image © gettyimages.com

Cover and text design by Katherine Robinson.

Printed and bound in the United States of America.

Library of Congress Cataloging-in-Publication Data is available.

To my parents, Maria and Denis McGuire.
With deep gratitude for the lifetime
of love and support that you have given me.

To all of the friends and mentors who have journeyed
alongside me and have been a voice of hope, support, and
encouragement in my life. You have taught me what it means
to be faithful.

To Jake, Maria, Judah, and Eva. I love you.

To our God and Father be glory forever and ever. Amen.
—Philippians 4:20

CONTENTS

FOREWORD

I continue to be amazed—no, that's not the right word; saddened, yes, that's the word—saddened at the number of Christians who don't live life to the fullest.

Jesus said in John's gospel that he came so we may have life and have it abundantly. "Abundant life" is such a wonderful image; it speaks to fullness, completeness, freedom, and wholeness—all qualities Jesus desires us to experience. God doesn't want us to merely dream about freedom, hope, and healing; rather, he wants us to experience these things in the deepest recesses of our souls. But sadly, too many Catholics are not experiencing this. So many feel as if they are constantly treading water, trying to catch their breath and merely surviving. The individuals are all around us; they fill our churches and our schools. I suppose at one time or another this is everyone's experience.

However, frustratingly, most people are not even aware there is another way to live. They have grown accustomed to getting by. They make comments like "It's not that bad" or "I'm okay, certainly better than John and Jane down the street," and they go on getting by. They hide things well, mask their struggles, and keep pushing on, to a prize they honestly are not 100 percent convinced is worth it. That's the part that is so tiring. They keep trying, running, fighting, and wanting life to magically be different; it's all so exhausting. And then, many just give up. It's just not possible or is too difficult, and they stop dreaming, hoping, and praying.

It doesn't have to be that way. There is a different way, a better way; it is *the* way. In *Abide: A Pathway to Transformative Healing and Intimacy with Jesus*, Heather Khym leads the reader to Jesus, the source of healing and wholeness. Heather invites the reader into a new way of living where the individual's life is marked by the work of God. Heather believes that Jesus' death, resurrection, and sending of his Holy Spirit should have an impact on every Christian. The grace and healing presence of Jesus is not something simply relegated to thousands of years ago; rather, God is working in the hearts of believers if he is invited.

In sharing her personal experiences of healing as well as what she's learned from a countless number of men and women she has led in their journey of healing, Heather beautifully presents a path to healing and freedom that is accessible and filled with hope. She shares her heart and witnesses to what Jesus has done for her, and I am certain this will inspire the same grace in the reader. The journey to healing is a deeply personal story, and for one to tell it well requires honesty, vulnerability, and courage—all virtues that Heather exhibits beautifully in sharing her story. She helps the reader to lean into God's grace, look at their own life, and see where God wants to bring healing. And instead of leaving readers there, she continues to guide them to a place of healing.

I appreciate how Heather is practical in her approach, instilling confidence that a new life in Christ is actually possible. The questions and suggestions she offers at the end of each chapter are extremely helpful in the work that God will do in the heart of the reader.

I've walked with Heather for more than twenty years and rejoice in what God has done in her life. I'm so excited that she is now sharing this with the world and am sure her story will lead many more men and women to a transforming encounter with Jesus the Christ.

Fr. Dave Pivonka, TOR
President of Franciscan University of Steubenville

INTRODUCTION

The thief comes only to steal and kill and destroy;
I came that they may have life, and have it abundantly.
John 10:10

An abundant life. Sounds awesome, doesn't it? We all want it, Jesus promised it, but I actually don't know too many people who would describe their life as abundant, as an experience of living life to the fullest. More often than not, our experience is that life is hard. I mean, I know we need to look on the bright side and there is so much to be grateful for. I know. But can we be honest? Life is still hard, and sometimes it's really hard. We don't usually like to admit it, but if we were to be vulnerable and take the lid off for a second, it would reveal that under the surface many of us are dealing with an incredible amount of pain, fear, disappointment, unmet desires, aches, anguish in relationships, longing, and mostly we are tired . . . so tired.

Much of this we can blame on our culture: we are constantly expected to be "on"—always at the mercy of responding to a hundred texts and emails a day, answering to the demands of life, putting on a good face for the family, for work, for our church communities, but underneath all of that, most people I talk to are downright exhausted and suffering. Maybe it's not immediately under the surface for you: maybe it's been buried under years of coping and surviving, but it's there. Is this really what Jesus meant when he said, "I came that they may have life, and have it abundantly" (Jn 10:10)?

Many of us have heard that scripture from the Gospel of John, and we want to believe it, but we don't actually know how to live an abundant life. It feels like an elusive promise that we can't seem to grasp with our hands and make a reality on this side of heaven. Thus, many of us end up trying to white-knuckle it through the hardships of life with the coping skills we need to function. The result is that most people feel they are living a mediocre life at best.

The question is, what if God's promises are real? What if we could truly live a life of abundance as we abide in him? What if God really is who he says he is? What if the same Jesus who healed the blind man, cleansed the leper, and raised Lazarus from the dead wants to and can perform powerful miracles that we desperately desire in our life as well? All of these questions rolled around in my heart for a long time, and they were unsettling. Either this was all true, and I didn't have a clue how to access it, or it wasn't true and my whole faith in God was a sham. I needed to know: Was there more to life than I was experiencing? Was the full life that Christ promised possible?

I have been Catholic my entire life, I have gone to Mass almost every Sunday, I studied theology at university, and I have worked in the Church since I was eighteen years old, but after all that, I was still unsure if Jesus could truly transform my life, the effects of my past, and set me free on this side of heaven. Somehow, I believed that bad things happen to us on this earth, and we just have to manage it as best we can until we, God willing, reach heaven. I completely missed the message that God wants to bring healing and restoration to our lives *here and now*. The more I talked with other Catholics about this, I realized it wasn't just me; this was surprisingly common among the faithful.

All of my questions came to a critical point when I was twenty-seven years old and my marriage was shaken to the core by the discovery of my husband's addiction and realization that our relationship was deeply broken. I knew I was unable to fix it on my own, and I had no choice but to find out if God really was the Divine Healer, the Restorer, and a miracle worker—not in general for the world but personally, for me. Was he my healer, my restorer, and a miracle worker in the circumstances of my life? All of my questions were about to be tested. Was all that I professed to believe every Sunday really true? Could the power of Jesus really change my life?

Through the process of being completely honest and entering into the healing journey, everything began to change. It was as if the scales were falling from my eyes until, suddenly, I could see. The healing power of God broke through my half-hearted living and radically changed me and has continued to bear good fruit to this day. I woke up to the truth that God *really is* who he says he is. Jesus began working miracles in my life, restoring what had been lost in my marriage and throughout various wounded places in my past. He also revealed several practical tools that I believe to be critical in the healing journey.

Through personal stories, scriptural truth, and Church teaching, this book offers a reintroduction to the truth of who we are, the truth of who God is, and some practical tools for living a restored life in Jesus. It's an opportunity to remove the fog and gain a clear perspective again, to discover a renewed hope in the power of God to heal even our deepest wounds. We all have parts of our lives and stories where we need a personal encounter with the real person of Jesus. The reality is that many hurdles are standing in our way—from doubt to a lack of self-awareness, a misunderstanding of who Jesus is, and the role of the enemy. These are blocks to our freedom; they hinder our ability to see the true Jesus.

It is easy underestimate how the events of our lives affect our understanding of God and, as a result, empower the enemy who, "like a roaring lion, your adversary the devil, prowls around looking for someone to devour" (1 Pt 5:8). When we come to an understanding that the enemy is real and how he works in our lives, we are able to stand up and fight in the spiritual battle. When we understand the blocks that are standing in the way of us and freedom, we can work through removing them and find the pathway to new life. Throughout these pages, you will have the opportunity to grow in the understanding of your unique story within the larger context of salvation history and where you need healing, restoration, and freedom in the broken places of your life.

Above all, a personal encounter with Jesus remains the source of our healing. This encounter is not supposed to be fleeting or one-and-done; it is steady, consistent. The daily living of the moment by moment together is what leads to intimacy and learning how to abide in him. Jesus says to us,

> Abide in me as I abide in you. Just as the branch cannot bear fruit by itself unless it abides in the vine, neither can you unless you abide in me. I am the vine, you are the branches. Those who abide in me and I in them bear much fruit because apart from me you can do nothing. (Jn 15:4–5)

We see in the words of Jesus that we were not meant to live life alone and apart from him. There is so much peace and joy to be found in abiding in Jesus. So, you see, the journey of healing isn't just a theoretical concept but something to be lived with practical tools. As you will learn in the pages of this book, we begin our healing with reorienting ourselves with our story, by encountering the true person of Jesus, acknowledging our brokenness, and abiding in the love of Jesus. For your journey, I've offered reflection questions and interactive charts to aid you in further reflection and growth in self-awareness and have also highlighted key italicized text to help draw your attention to concepts and truths I believe are of particular importance. Bear in mind that even with the best tools, the path to healing isn't fast and it isn't a onetime thing. Each layer of our lives needs the healing hand of God; therefore, I hope this book can be a manual of sorts that can be accessed again and again as you continue the journey to wholeness.

We were made for more. We were not meant to live a mediocre life; rather, we were meant to live a life of abundance in Jesus, abiding in him at every moment. I hope this book is a catalyst for you to enter into or continue the pathway of healing that leads to freedom. The world desperately needs people who have been restored by the power of Jesus, people who can proclaim this message to others. This is how we will restore the Church and the world;

it must begin within us.

Chapter 1

OUR BEGINNING AND OUR END

The Fog

We used to live in a beautiful little neighborhood up on a mountainside. Every morning when I drove the kids to school, we would descend the mountain and see the most glorious view: the sun would rise behind a beautiful snow-capped mountain, and a lovely valley of trees sat at its feet. We would always comment on how amazing and different it looked each morning depending on how the light hit, the clouds broke open, or the streaks of pink and orange would shoot across the sky. The beauty we encountered those mornings was a gift to my soul and something God continually used to speak to me and teach me lessons.

One morning was particularly stunning. The sky was a vivid blue, without a cloud in sight. The sun shone bright above the majestic mountain, causing the snow caps to sparkle like diamonds. At the base of the mountain was a thick blanket of fog covering the whole valley. The way the sun hit the fog made it look like the ocean shimmering below it. I've never seen anything like it—it took my breath away.

As we drove down the hill, the fog soon enveloped us. The sun disappeared quickly, and the fog was so thick I couldn't see more than two feet in front of or behind my car. The bright morning had suddenly turned dark and misty, and I thought, if I only lived in the valley below, I would never have known the sun was shining above and was going to burn away the fog and that the day ahead would be full of beauty and wonder. It was at that moment I heard the Lord speak gently to my heart. He said:

> Pay attention to this, Heather. You often live your life like this, with very little perspective. You don't live with a strong vision of where you've come from and where you're going. *Most days you live in a fog, and I'm inviting you to lift your eyes higher so you can see things from a kingdom perspective.* I need for you to always carry with you the knowledge of where you have come from and where you are going.

This gentle encounter with the Lord set me on a path of reorienting myself to the larger story of salvation. That path led me to reencounter the Gospel with a new perspective, where I started to understand salvation history as *my* history and my own personal life as a part of the larger story that God was writing.

We all need a shift in our perspective, a shift from the natural to the supernatural. It's easy for us to look around and see and interpret the world through our own experiences, emotions, and beliefs about our life. We see a series of joys, sorrows, wins, losses, relationships, successes, failures, and so on. It's much harder to look at these same things and see the meaning and purpose through the lens of faith, through a kingdom perspective, and in the context of the greater story that God is writing. We often look at life in the context of what we are dealing with and experiencing right now, but there is a much larger story happening and we are right in the middle of it.

It is vitally important that we reengage with what we think we already know about the story of God and open our hearts to hear it again with new ears and find out the new things God wants to reveal to us. A shift in perspective and a broadening in our understanding of what our life is all about, where we have come from, and our destination are essential in the journey of restoration. It will give us a compass to navigate our past, our present, and our future. So, let's begin to clear the fog by reorienting ourselves with the simple truths we often overlook.

God is love. I have heard this thousands of times throughout my life, but for years I didn't quite make the connection that if God is love (see 1 John 4:16), and we are made in his image (see Genesis 1:27), then we are made in the image of Love. Love! Isn't this what we all crave more than anything? To love and be loved? The reason this ache is so deep within us is that love is the image in which we were made. We were made out of Love, for Love, and to be in perfect union with Love forever. Well, that sounds like the best news I've ever heard! Why, then, does that good news seem to stay lost somewhere in the back of my mind and not at the forefront where it can influence the moment by moment of each day? Why does a fog descend into my heart and cause me to lose my way so often? What if that could change? How would my life be different if I lived with clarity and that perspective in my mind and heart daily?

> If we don't know where we have come
> from and where we are going, it's very
> difficult to navigate the middle—and the
> middle is our entire life on earth.

Scripture is one of the most important places of truth that we can look to for clarity because it is God's own Word revealed to us, and he doesn't lie. We often look at scripture as a rather daunting book, filled with good ideas and lessons, but mostly ones we don't understand, and we struggle to see how they all relate to our daily life. In order for scripture to take on a personal quality for us, we need to ask the Holy Spirit to come and illuminate our hearts and minds with his truth.

When scripture is experienced for what it really is, it changes everything. It isn't a boring, old, irrelevant book; on the contrary, this is the greatest love story ever told and still unfolding, the truest story to which every other great story points. This is why good books and movies stir our hearts so deeply: they echo the story of our salvation history and what has been written in the core of our hearts as human beings. Within the pages of scripture, we see love, deception, war, healing, infidelity, restoration, adventure, courage, sorrow, romance, loss, and triumph. Do you experience scripture like this when you read it? Let's pause for a moment and pray.

Come Holy Spirit and illuminate my mind and heart to understand the scriptures, the story of my salvation history, with clarity and power. Speak life and truth into my very being and cause your Word to become real to me. Amen.

I'd love for you to join me on the journey back to the beginning and listen to our salvation history with new ears. Can I tell you a story?

The Love Story

In the beginning, God created Adam and Eve. Their story in Genesis tells us that Adam and Eve could hear God walking in the garden in the cool of the day. Could you imagine going into your backyard to walk and talk with God in the cool of the day? Life was perfect before the fall; everything was as it was meant to be and was in perfect harmony and union with God. There was no pain, no tears, no hiding, just perfect intimate love. This is what we were made for, and it was supposed to stay that way forever, but we all know that is not how the story goes. One of the greatest gifts God ever gave us is the gift of free will—the ability to choose for ourselves. If there was only one option and if we were forced to love God, then we wouldn't really be free and it wouldn't truly be love. God wants our relationship with him to be out of a place of freedom instead of an obligation.

In the Genesis story, we see the choices for Adam and Eve quickly appear. The enemy, in the form of the serpent, entered into the garden and began telling Adam and Eve lies, lies that caused them to question the very heart of God. For the first time, their trust in God was challenged, and doubt crept in. In their dialogue with the enemy, essential questions arose in their hearts and they wondered, "Is God really good? Was he holding something back from them by not letting them eat the fruit of the tree of the knowledge of good and evil? What if that fruit would make them even happier?" Here we see the fog and confusion start to settle into their hearts. They began to forget who God was, forget where they came from, forget that he was trustworthy, and desired their good even more than they did themselves. So, they chose to go their own way and ate the fruit, in search of something other than God to make them happy.

"They heard the sound of the Lord God walking in the garden at the time of the evening breeze, and the man and his wife hid themselves from the presence of the Lord God among the trees of the garden. But the Lord God called to the man, and said to him, '*Where are you?*' He said, 'I heard the sound of you in the garden, and I was afraid, because I was naked; and I hid myself' (Gn 3:8–10; emphasis mine)."

At that moment, a catastrophic rupture occurred in the relationship between God and humanity, and union with God was lost. In their deep shame, Adam and Eve hid and covered themselves. They were scared, they were embarrassed, they didn't want God to see them, and they likely didn't think he loved them enough to overcome their sin. God came to the garden to walk with them as he did each day, but this day, they were nowhere to be found.

The question in Genesis I find particularly beautiful is when God calls to them and asks, "Where are you?" as if he doesn't already know. Sometimes we can read a line in scripture like that and put a tone to God's voice based on the previous negative experiences we have had. We could interpret the voice of God saying those words harshly, with disdain, with disappointment, and with intent to shame them, but if we truly understand the heart of God and his desire for union, would he not have said it with gentleness, mercy, and love? Where are you my beloved ones?

The tone we apply to God's voice in scripture is important because this is

the tone we hear in God's voice when
he speaks to us in our lives.

When God saw Adam and Eve in their shame and the massive chasm of sin dividing them from himself, he immediately began to pursue them and the reunification of the relationship. There was no way for humanity to regain perfect union with God on our own. We were utterly lost. Only God could restore this; only God could save us because, as scripture says, "the wages of sin is death" (Rom 6:23). That was the only option for us; it was just and what we deserved. In this place of being completely helpless and doomed to die, we see the incredible heart of God. Filled with radical mercy, compassion, and faithful love, he refused to let us go. He would not let us be separated from him forever. Thus, the Father began his plan of restoration, to make a way and bring us back to himself, to close the gap between us and save us from being separated from Love for all eternity. He made an unbreakable covenant with us.

We see over and over again throughout the Old Testament the same cycle occurring. God makes a covenant and his people continue to fail; they are unfaithful, they go their own way, and through it all, God remains faithful. God's word is not like ours: what he says is always true, and when he makes a promise, he always comes through. God has been unrelenting in his pursuit of us and was always committed to being all in, even to the point of sending his own Son to die for us and pay the price we could not pay, so we could be restored to union with him. The culmination of his whole rescue plan was in the life, death, and resurrection of Jesus. "But he was wounded for our transgressions, crushed for our iniquities; upon him was the punishment that made us whole, and by his bruises we are healed" (Is 53:5).

Many of us have very little understanding of what this all means, yet this is the pinnacle of the entire story of our entire faith. It deserves regular, consistent pause and reflection, but most of all, it deserves a personal response from us. The whole story needs to move from the exterior to the interior, from being a story about someone else to internalizing it as your story and my story. Jesus didn't die just for the world; he died for me and he died for you, personally. Not only did the Israelites show infidelity to God, but I have and I still do. In my heart and in my life are similar stories as are written about in scripture, and when I'm honest, I am not the hero in those stories. I am the unfaithful one, I am the harlot, I am Pilate, I am the roman soldier, and that makes me desperately in need of a savior.

Here's the good news: we *already have* a savior. Our knowledge and experience of Jesus as Savior also needs to move from the exterior to the interior. He's not just a savior; he's your Savior. We don't need to go looking for him in earthly pleasures or worldly ideals. Jesus has already adopted us as sons and daughters through our Baptism. And his death on a cross for our individual sins deserves a personal response from each of us. I'd like to encourage you to pause for a moment. Is there anything stirring in your heart that you'd like to say to Jesus in response to his love? If you're not sure, that's okay. My hope is that throughout this book you will encounter Jesus in a more personal way and that a desire to respond to him would come naturally.

Heaven

In the book of Revelation, God promises that one day, we will have no more tears, no pain, no sorrow, and that all things will be made new. No shame, no rejection, no anger, no brokenness, no more aching. Our hearts, souls, bodies, and desires will be completely satisfied by the One whom we were meant to be with from the very beginning. God will be one with us again, and we will finally be *home*. Until that day comes, we are not meant to just suffer and white-knuckle it through life. We are invited to wait in joyful hope for the coming of Jesus, and while we wait, we will inevitably struggle, but we will also have opportunities to experience some of that unity now. We can be healed and restored now, and taste joy in living life to the full today: "I consider that the sufferings of this present time are not worth comparing with the glory about to be revealed to us" (Rom 8:18).

We all find ourselves experiencing the effects of the fall, places of disunity, and disintegration within our own hearts and relationship with God. The truth is that the same God who set out to rescue humanity is here to rescue *you*. He wants a perfect union with *you*. No hiding, no walls, no shame, nothing in between, and as vulnerable and maybe even scary as that may sound, this is the deepest desire written upon your heart, to be one with the One who made you, loves you, and knows you. He knows every hair on your head, the curve of your smile, the quirks in your personality, the aches in your heart, your strengths, your weaknesses, your pain, your passions, the things that make you come alive, your hunger and thirst for life to be amazing. He knows you more than you know yourself and he *chooses you*, he wants you. He always has and always will.

Pause now to connect with your story and the greater story of salvation. Are you willing to let the rescue of your heart begin? Are you open to hearing the voice of God call to you, as he did with Adam and Eve in the garden, "Where are you?" Friend, where are you right now? Where are you hiding? Why are you in the shadows? Isn't it exhausting and lonely there? Are you willing to be vulnerable and let him see you? Will you let yourself be found?

Pause & REFLECT

Take some time to journal and reflect on the following questions:

> What are the things in my life that create "the fog," the things that make it difficult to remember who I am and God's plan for me?

> What are the things I do or don't do that frequently cause a rupture in my relationship with God?

> When I think about heaven, what comes to mind?

> Am I ready to commit my life to Jesus and accept him as my Savior?

Slowly and thoughtfully pray these words:

Jesus, you are the Son of God and I believe in you. I believe you died for my sins and have made a way for me to be with you forever. I believe you want to heal and restore me. I want to come into the light of your presence and abide with you. I want to acknowledge that the story of salvation is my story. I am sorry, Lord, so sorry, for all the ways I have sinned against you. I ask your forgiveness for all the moments I have chosen to go my own way and turn away from you. Jesus, I want to commit my life to you; I choose you. I ask that you would come into my life and be my Lord and Savior. I pray that you would restore me, heal me, and set me free. I love you, I trust you, and I give my life to you. Amen.

Chapter 2

WE HAVE A STORY

When my son, Judah, was about two and a half years old, he woke up suddenly in the middle of the night and could barely breathe. Somehow, by God's grace, I woke up with a strange feeling, went into his room to check on him, and found him gasping for air—he couldn't get enough. It was as if he was breathing through a tiny straw. The color was draining in his face quickly, so I scooped him up and put him in our van as fast as I could. I buckled him in his car seat and began the eight-minute drive to the hospital. In about two minutes I realized I couldn't get him there in time, so I called 911.

They instructed me to quickly pull over in front of the nearest house with an address so they could find me. I felt so panicked but tried to remain outwardly calm for Judah. When I pulled over, I unbuckled my son and lifted him into the front seat onto my lap. I rolled the window down in hopes that the cool air would help open his airways. I was staring into his big brown eyes, and they were locked on me, his grip tightening on my hand as he struggled to get air. I felt so afraid and helpless; my son was dying, and there was nothing I could do but wait.

The street I pulled over on was on the side of a mountain, and in the distance, I started to hear the faint sounds of an ambulance siren rising. My heart quickened as I realized they were for him. I looked at my sweet boy with tears in my eyes and said, "Judah, do you hear that? Buddy, they are coming for you; they are coming to save you." Within moments bright lights blazed in our face as the ambulance and fire truck full of first responders rounded the corner. They jumped out, grabbed Judah, and gave him a steroid and oxygen immediately to help him breathe. I felt utter relief when they arrived because they were capable of something I wasn't. They rescued him; they saved my boy.

I've thought about that moment a lot, so grateful there was someone who could save Judah's life when I couldn't. In prayer one day, the Lord drew my attention back to that moment and showed me that all of us find ourselves in a similar position in life. We are going through life, but there are places where we are barely breathing, hardly surviving, and we are incapable of doing anything to save ourselves. In his wisdom and love, God has given us the Church and sacred scripture to be like a siren, a prophetic voice in the world that is speaking loudly to all who are in despair and need that the Savior has come and is coming back again. The essential thing we need to understand is that

---

if we can't see the deep brokenness in the story of our own lives, the places we need to be saved, then we won't experience our deep need for a Savior,

and we likely won't allow Jesus to save
us and set us free.

Funnily enough, we are great at convincing ourselves that barely breathing is sufficient, maybe even that it's normal. We convince ourselves that this "just surviving" way of living is as good as it gets, so we lower our expectations of the goodness of life and the goodness of God that we are invited to experience now. But friends, you were made for more than this. You were made to thrive and have joy flooding your heart! You were made to taste sweetness and experience the deep passion of this life while living in the anticipation of the fulfillment of our hope in the next life. Jesus didn't come so we could have a mediocre existence and cope; rather, he said to us, "I have come that you might have life and have it to the fullest" (Jn 10:10). It is only in understanding our full story, in light of a God who loves us, that we can see what has been missed, what has been lost, and what God wants to restore.

In the previous chapter, we got oriented to the larger story of salvation. We went back to the very beginning with Adam and Eve, sin, and the rupture of our relationship with God because, when we understand that, we can make sense of why Jesus had to come and understand where we are headed. The next important step is to recognize that with the larger story of salvation, each of us has a personal story and that story matters. We will begin to see how the overarching story of salvation is mirrored in our individual narratives. Just like salvation history, our personal story is also filled with moments of love, pain, deception, battles, healing, infidelity, restoration, adventure, courage, sorrow, romance, loss, and triumph, and it also has the Savior.

Just as Adam and Eve had a significant moment of wounding in their lives and relationship with God and the enemy
actively pursuing their demise, so do we. Each of us has been
wounded throughout our lives and has heard the voice of the
serpent whispering similar lies in our hearts, such as, "Is God
really real? Is he really good? Does he really care? Is he keeping
good things from me? Can I really trust him?" If we begin to
see where the lies began, then we can invite Jesus in to speak the
truth and experience God's restoring power. We must begin to
look at our life story with new eyes and see that our past directly
affects who we are and our struggles today.

The powerful film *Good Will Hunting* speaks to the reality of
a person struggling from the effects of their past.[1] Will, the main
character, has quite a life story. He seems to mostly be a good
guy, loyal to his friends, hardworking, and protective of those he
loves, but when pressed the wrong way, he can be mean, cutting,
and cold, and push people away, while maintaining a disposition of being unaffected. As the movie progresses, we learn that
Will had experienced horrible trauma in his childhood. The
physical and emotional abuse from his father had wounded
him so deeply that although he acted as if he had moved on and
gotten over it, it became clear that his actions in his present life
were being dramatically affected, almost controlled, by his past.

In one pivotal moment, he was talking with a young woman
he was romantically involved with and loved very much. When
the conversation got too vulnerable, he started to shut down
and create distance from her. At one point she tells him that if
he doesn't love her, to just say it, and she will leave him alone.
She stands before him with tears in her eyes and a heart full
of love, aching for his response. Instead of drawing close, as
he desperately wanted to, he looks her dead in the eyes and

tells her he doesn't love her. My heart cringed when he said it. The pain on her face was deep, while he looked empty and unmoved.

The truth is that inside of Will was an abyss of pain, but he had disconnected from his feelings and piled so much self-protection on top of it that he couldn't sort out what was in his heart or how to let his guard down. He lied when he said he didn't love her. The truth was that he loved her more than anyone, but the fear of vulnerability and being hurt was too much of a risk, so he pushed her away in order to protect and give himself a sense of safety. He believed that if he was alone, kept up his tough facade, and stuck to the things that had worked for him in the past, then he couldn't be hurt, but something had changed. In the presence of someone who really loved him, he couldn't hide from the truth that was beginning to gently ring in his heart.

In the past, he had always shut people out and could cope with the loss, but this time, it wasn't going to work because he didn't want to lose her. He wanted to protect himself, but he didn't want to push her away, and he realized he couldn't do both. If he desired to be with her, he needed to choose a new path, live a new way, to be able to have the life he really wanted.

At particular moments in our lives, we become aware that the things we have used in the past to keep ourselves safe aren't going to work in the future.

Will is no different than any of us. We all have a story, we all have a past, and whether we realize it or not, it comes out in our present moments, thought patterns, emotions, and responses.

Maybe our past is similar to Will's, or maybe we believe we don't have anything dramatic enough to have affected us. *Whatever your story holds, it matters.* Every part, whether it seems significant or not, makes us who we are today, for better or worse. Our actions, or lack of action, our words, our thought patterns, the lies we believe, and the narrative going on in our mind seem to be connected to the present alone, but the truth is it is mixed up with wounds and pain from our past.

This mental battle engages questions about our identity, safety, worth, belonging, lack of control, ability to succeed, and lovability. The battle often presents itself in our lives through relationship disruptions, misunderstandings, judgments, exerting control, depression, anxiety, addictions, settling, busyness, numbing, dissociating, self-harm, reckless behavior, impulsivity, shame, performing for attention, neediness, unhealthy sexual behavior, abandonment, and many other forms.

When we come to discover our story, we can find the roots of many patterns of behavior and thoughts that we carry in our current stage of life, and just like a tree, the health of the roots determines the health of the tree and the fruit. Whatever ways you've been hurt by others in your past, it's not your fault. You didn't choose to be hurt, and you have never deserved to be treated with anything other than love, care, and tenderness. You also have the opportunity to experience freedom from the effects of your past and the ways you have learned to cope with the pain.

In my own story, I have significant places of pain, abuse, abandonment, trauma, and fear. The interesting thing is that I had no idea how it was all connected until I was in my thirties. Maybe I compartmentalized it or convinced myself I was over it, but more likely than not, I dissociated from the whole thing because I was traumatized and I wanted to protect myself. Dissociation is something our minds do in response to traumatic events. We internally shut down to protect ourselves from the pain or memories we have experienced, so we don't have to hurt or feel afraid anymore. When someone dissociates, they can experience things like a numbing of their emotions, gaps in their memory, deep denial that anything even happened, or a glossed-over view of their past that makes it seem better than it was. For myself, I did all of the above.

I didn't realize it, but for many years, when I was asked about my family, I would say things like "Oh I have a great family; I'm super blessed" or "We have had such a good life, and we are all really close." Many friends would come in and out of our home and experience love, connection, and care in ways that made them wish they could have a family like that or parents like mine. Some even jokingly referred to us as a "Beaver Cleaver" family, insinuating that it was happy-go-lucky and picture-perfect. Everyone was always welcome at my house, and I often came home to my friends sitting on the kitchen counter eating fresh-baked cookies while chatting with my mom. We faithfully went to church each Sunday and were involved in different ministries and charitable organizations. It was easy to believe all was well; in fact, I had even convinced myself this was true.

Don't get me wrong—my family was full of love, strong relationships, and tenderness, but from the outside, no one could see the pain under the surface. They couldn't see all the trauma and brokenness in our history that had affected each member of the family and how individually we were trying to cope with it in unhealthy ways, such as overworking, staying too busy, harmful attachments to food and alcohol, drug abuse, numbing ourselves, and staying emotionally guarded.

I know it sounds funny, but I had blocked out so much of my own story (disassociation) that I unknowingly took on a false narrative about my family life that included only the good aspects and ignored the hard ones. But when I was able to be honest with myself, the memory of those really painful moments of emotional and psychological abuse felt like a movie or someone else's story, rather than my own real life. I had disassociated from the trauma, from the pain, and in doing so, closed those parts of my heart to Jesus.

I was living in a fog. The moment that broke through that fog came one day when I was in my kitchen with my daughter, Maria. I looked over at her, eleven years old at the time, the exact age I was when most of my trauma happened. For the first time I thought, "Oh my gosh, that's how old I was when all those bad things happened to me. She's so little and innocent. What if those things happened to her?" My heart just began to break at the thought of her or any child going through what I went through. For the first time, I felt compassion for myself, and the shift in perspective allowed me to grasp the gravity of what had happened to me.

As I began a journey of healing from my traumatic past, which I will discuss more in chapter 3, my initial response was a deep feeling of guilt. I felt so guilty about acknowledging these places of pain and failure within my family relationships because, in comparison to other people, I had a really good life and so many blessings. I didn't feel I had the right to complain. I had loving parents, and even my relationships with my siblings had changed so much for the better that it seemed really ungrateful and dishonoring to go back in and focus on the past faults and hurts. In an unhealthy way, I wanted to "protect" my family at the expense of my own healing.

I didn't understand that diving into the pain of my story and family was an opportunity for healing the sinful parts that God did not intend for anyone, not taking away or diminishing the beautiful parts. I remember struggling with this one day and felt the Lord gently say to me, "Heather, I don't want you to compare your pain to anyone else. Yes, there are many people who have experienced worse things than you, but this is painful *for you* and I want to heal *you*. I don't want you to carry this pain anymore; I want to set you free." These words from the Lord allowed me to let my guard of protection down, my guard of not wanting to be ungrateful, and allowed me to look honestly at my own life story that included hurt and pain. I wasn't looking to blame anyone; this was an opening to the truth.

Looking at our pain doesn't negate the good that was there; it holds the good steady, while it opens the door for healing of the places that weren't what should have been.

We can react in a thousand different ways to our past wounds, but there are four very common reactions I'd like to explore with you: diminishment, dissociation, perpetual victimhood, and naivete.

Diminishment

The first is to downplay the severity of the events and hold a belief that the past is in the past and we should just get over it. The truth is that our past pain unexpectedly launches into our present moments all the time. It's called a trigger. For example, I was watching a movie the other night where a younger boy was sitting in a room alone and in pain; suddenly tears began to slide down my cheeks as old feelings and memories of me being alone and in pain with no one to help me came rushing in. The movie was the trigger that launched the feeling of the past into the present.

After doing a lot of my own healing work, I'm now aware enough to know where those feelings came from, but if you haven't pressed into your story, you likely experience a variety of emotions and assume they are just about the present without knowing what the root is in the past. Sometimes you'll hear an adult say to another adult in frustration, "Why are you acting like an eight-year-old right now?" Well, it's likely because an eight-year-old part of that person was hurt at some point, has been triggered by a current event, and is now right under the surface.

We all have these little places within us, old places where we are young, where we are stuck in some kind of pain, so it's actually impossible to "just get over it." We may have told ourselves that this is exactly what we have done, but it's simply not true. *We can stuff pain, but we can't just get over it.* It's important to switch from stuffing those memories and emotions down and invite Jesus to show us what is happening within our hearts. Our current negative reactions are likely coming from an old unhealed place, and our current positive and healthy reactions are coming from places in our past where we were loved well or are now healed.

Being healed and getting over it is not
the same thing.

Dissociation

The second common reaction we can have to our past wounds is acting as though it didn't happen by blocking out bad memories or stifling them with whatever coping mechanism we have learned along the way. When we do this, we experience a lack of integration within ourselves and often can't make sense of our own inner world. We find it hard to know why we do what we do or even what we need. We explain away our unhealthy behavior by saying things like "This is just who I am" instead of growing aware that there are reasons for our actions and we can change. We are dramatically affected by our environment, and if that environment was unhealthy, we will likely have a lot of unhealthy places within us. Although not our fault, we do suffer from our past; it might come out in addictions, sin, or trouble connecting or keeping relationships, but rest assured it will come out somehow. Asking Jesus to shine the light of his love to expose what is in the areas we can't see is an important step in knowing our story. Believing he can make all things new is the hope we can cling to.

Perpetual Victimhood

The third common reaction is that we realize the truth that we were victims, but instead of seeking healing, we stay a victim and allow our past wounds to become our identity and define who we are. I know several people who have experienced severe abuse in their past, and they have been able to heal and move into a new place of freedom, but I know many more people in a similar situation who continue to be traumatized every day by those events. The enemy wants us to believe we are the culmination of our wounds and are nothing more than our shortcomings, but the truth is that no matter what has happened to us and what we have done, we are beloved sons and daughters of God. As Pope John Paul II said, "We are not the sum of our weaknesses and failures; we are the sum of the Father's love for us."[2]

We have all been victims of hurt and pain, but we are not meant to stay there. God desires to heal and restore so we can become a witness to the Good News of the saving power of Jesus for others who are still victims. As we heal, we can bring the message of hope for others. Scripture tells us, "Know that I am with you and will keep you wherever you go, and will bring you back to this land; for I will not leave you until I have done what I have promised you" (Gn 28:15), and "after you have suffered for a little while, the God of all grace, who has called you to his eternal glory in Christ, will himself restore, support, strengthen, and establish you" (1 Pt 5:10).

Naivete

Fourth, we don't fully understand our wounds and are blind to the ways we are suffering and the healing God desires for us. The family we grew up in is all we know, and therefore that becomes our idea of normal. We may see signs of something different in healthier families, but we don't know what it's like to grow up in that environment, which makes it very difficult to see the impact of what we should have had and what we didn't get. When we don't have a healthy understanding of what a human person needs and deserves to thrive, we can't clearly see the impact of what we received and didn't receive along the way. Coming into the awareness of the truth of what human beings deserve and need to thrive—what you deserve and need to thrive—is essential to see where we have deficiencies and what we need God to heal within us.

Again, this isn't stirring things up for the sake of creating more pain; rather, it's bringing in the truth and light of God so we can experience the fullness of life and healing that he intends for us. We are meant to be free, and God the Father wants to fill in all the gaps of what we didn't get and maybe still aren't getting through our families and relationships.

All four of these reactions lead us to believing that either we don't need a Savior or we don't have a Savior who can truly save us and set us free. The truth is,

---

we all need Jesus, and he is
powerful enough to heal anything
and everything.

No matter what your story holds in its pages—the pain, the trauma, the unseen, the secrets, or even the seemingly uneventful—your story matters, and God has more for you. In our hearts we have aches and longings that cannot be satisfied by anyone or anything other than Jesus, so despite the brokenness of our past, Jesus was and still is the only answer; he was and still is the only One who will fully satisfy the longing for love, belonging, and relationship we all have, and he wants to do so. The following quote from St. John Paul II has been a source of inspiration and truth for me since I was young. It has been a reminder to me not to settle for anything less than the full life God intends for us and keeps me focused on the pursuit of restoration.

> It is Jesus that you seek when you dream of happiness; He
> is waiting for you when nothing else you find satisfies you;
> He is the beauty to which you are so attracted; it is He who
> provoked you with that thirst for fullness that will not let

you settle for compromise; it is He who urges you to shed the masks of a false life; it is He who reads in your heart your most genuine choices, the choices that others try to stifle. It is Jesus who stirs in you the desire to do something great with your lives, the will to follow an ideal, the refusal to allow yourselves to be ground down by mediocrity, the courage to commit yourselves humbly and patiently to improving yourselves and society, making the world more human and more fraternal.[3]

The importance of understanding our story and the impact of our wounds cannot be understated. It might be hard, and it might cause pain, but the hope is that it will lead to resurrection and new life in Jesus. The reality is, we are already in pain and are likely numbing or avoiding it. We are invited to wake up to our own life and the power of God to heal and restore it.

Pause & REFLECT

Take some time to journal and reflect on the following questions:

Who are the main characters in your life story?

Who had a positive impact on your life? Who had a negative impact on your life?

What is one negative and one positive event from your past that you would say changed everything?

Chapter 3

WE HAVE AN ENEMY

I am the youngest of four children. I have an older sister and two brothers, one of whom passed away when he was seven years old and I was just a baby. My parents raised us in the Catholic faith, and we went to Mass every week, received the sacraments, and had a Catholic education. I often trailed behind my mom to many a prayer meeting or pro-life event. Although I attended these events, to be honest it wasn't personal for me. I liked the idea of God and believed he was real, but the idea of the devil or a spiritual enemy sounded more like a fairytale than reality.

In my younger years, my dad ran a successful business, and my mom's incredible gift of hospitality made our home a warm and welcoming place for everyone we knew. The door was always open, so coming home to warm cookies and people visiting was a regular occasion in my house. I loved it. Often people would look at our family with envy because they thought things were perfect. I think this is a common experience, but although things can look put together on the outside, every person and every family has wounds, brokenness, suffering, and pain under the surface that few can see or understand. As human beings, we are good at hiding and even better at coping and covering up our unresolved pain.

We all have parts of our life that are in the light and other parts that are hidden in the dark.

The truth was that although my family had a lot of great qualities and there is so much I am grateful for, like most families, we were no strangers to pain and suffering. Traumatic events hit each of my family members in a variety of ways. Sexual, emotional, and physical abuse, extreme poverty, the death of a child, bullying, violence, addiction, and abandonment hurt us.

When I was about eleven years old, my sixteen-year-old brother got involved in the occult. Despite our strong Catholic upbringing and our faithfully praying mother, my brother ended up in a very dark place. His own unresolved trauma left him grasping for power and control, which made the occult very enticing to him. His experience was less about worshipping Satan and much more about having power and dominance over people. Before long, he was filled with rage and anger and got into frequent fights and trouble.

I was the younger sister and sadly the easiest target for him to exert his twisted power and control over. He hid an Ouija board in the house and cast demonic curses on people, all the while holding me hostage in our own home through fear, terrorization, and intimidation. Along with persistent humiliation

27

and bullying, he told me about many dark and horrible spiritual things he was a part of and often threatened to end my life if I were to ever tell anyone. Although my mom was very close to me and would ask me regularly what was wrong, I couldn't tell her. I was trapped in a painful cycle of psychological, emotional, and spiritual abuse but was threatened by force into silence, so I didn't tell a soul.

The enemy often likes to work in the dark, in secrets, in our isolation—that is his playground.

Needless to say, I soon found myself lying awake every night, all night, for two years paralyzed by fear. Not only was my awareness of the evil surrounding me increasing, but also I had begun to visibly see demonic spirits, in the form of shadows, moving around my house while everyone was asleep, and unfortunately it wasn't my imagination. The terror of evil gripped me as I became suddenly aware that evil was in my home, and I was all alone. I felt like a prisoner to my fear of the devil, and every time I cried out to God for help, it seemed to fall on deaf ears.

It was in those long, lonely nights as an eleven-year-old that a very powerful lie from the enemy took root in my heart: "God is very far away, and although he could help me, he won't. He's just coldly watching from a distance, unwilling to save me." It was as if the enemy was whispering this lie to me about God being distant and uncaring, and in my mind, I agreed with him and said in my heart, "Yeah, that feels true. God *is* distant and not willing to protect me."

When we agree with a lie from the
enemy, it plants a negative seed in our
heart, and the longer it stays there, the
deeper the roots grow and the more
negative fruit it will bear. The reality is
that the devil is our enemy, he is a liar,
and we have all made agreements with
him and his lies in one way or another.

Over the course of a couple of years, I went from a happy-
go-lucky kid to a very wounded, broken, and insecure teenager.
If I didn't believe the enemy was real before, I believed it now.
The negative fruit that came from the root lie that God was
distant and uncaring showed up in a variety of ways but pri-
marily in the beliefs that no one would protect me, that I had
to take care of everything myself, and that safety was all up to
me. I unknowingly vowed to be the strong one, to take care of
all the people around me, and also to practice intense vigilance
by watching out for all the darkness and evil that I believed
was lurking around every corner. I didn't consciously know
this was happening, and it wasn't until much later that I had
the perspective to see it. It's hard to see the reality and effects
of events in our lives while it's happening.

Perspective almost always comes in
hindsight.

Later I found out that my mother was waking up through
the night to intercede for my brother and was praying for

protection over all of us. Although she didn't know what I was going through, she knew the enemy was at work and was doing intense spiritual warfare. Finally, after a few years of experiencing trauma from my brother, my prayerful mother, by the grace of God, finally had a powerful intervention with him and he began to change. The traumatic environment changed, but the effects the trauma had on me didn't. The terror and self-protection raged within my heart and my memories. Damage was done, roots were deep, negative fruit was growing, and I was doing my best to shove it all down as far as I could by trying to forget and move on.

This is usually where most of us stay. We learn how to cope with our pain, but we don't usually know how to experience true healing and freedom from our pain. Our attempts at coping and the inability to heal ourselves can take many forms in our life and can manifest in things like control, emotional disconnect, victimhood, overachieving, addiction, gluttony, chaos, depression, anxiety, busyness, the need for constant attention, the need to always be right, sleeplessness, physical pain, and many others. We usually live our lives with very little understanding of why we do what we do or how we can get out of unhealthy situations.

As I grew up and as my life expanded, so did my responsibilities. I went to university, got married and had three children, began working in full-time church ministry, and did my best to keep everything under control with a heavy lid on the pain. Along with many people around me, I saw myself as strong, independent, and capable. I juggled, handled, hustled, and took care of it all—at least that's what I thought was happening. By the time I turned thirty, my life began to unravel. What felt like a switch that had suddenly flipped leaving me powerless to all the hidden realities I now see had been a slow unraveling to a breaking point. Seemingly from out of nowhere, I began suffering from intense physical pain, dizziness, anxiety, and depression. My ability to control and handle life by myself was declining at a rapid pace.

Within a few months, I was curled up on the couch, unable to move, and feeling like a very scared and dependent child. In hindsight, I have realized it's because in certain places of my heart I was afraid and little. I didn't know it at the time, but *there had always been a part of me that was a scared and dependent child.* That eleven-year-old part of me that was terrorized by my brother never grew up, and I had covered her up with the false mask of strength and control. Just like Adam and Eve in the garden, I was afraid, because I was vulnerable, so I hid.

We have all inherited the sin of
self-reliance from Adam and Eve.
These ancient coping mechanisms
are active within all of us.

After two years of praying and struggling to keep my head above water with the debilitating emotional, spiritual, and physical issues, I decided I needed to get away with my husband and be with a few of my closest friends, one of whom was a priest I had known since I was fourteen years old. These were people who knew me; they knew my story and loved me and were ready to battle for my freedom.

The experience of being around
people who knew me and knew my

> story brought a level of safety that
> was necessary to let down my walls of
> self-protection.

For the first time, I was desperate enough and ready to let people really care for me. Through my time with them, I encountered the healing power of God in such a deep way that it literally changed my whole life.

When I arrived at the airport in Boise, Idaho, I was met with hugs and smiles. Fr. Justin put his arm in mine and said he would like to pray a healing Mass for me. My immediate reaction was to say no, but I caught myself and remembered that now was the time to let my guard down and let other people care for me. Having a priest present and active in pursuing my freedom was a huge gift.

> Although we can experience healing
> in a variety of ways, there are some
> aspects of healing that God has
> ordained to come through the Church,
> the sacraments, and the power of the
> priesthood.

The Mass he prayed for me was so powerful that it ushered in a radical encounter with God.

After Mass, I was sitting on a couch, and Fr. Justin came over and stood in front of me; he laid his hands on my head and began praying an old prayer of the Church for healing and deliverance. As he prayed, I began to tremble. I don't know how else to describe it other than the power of Christ came through the prayers and through Fr. Justin's anointed hands. The power working through his priesthood was so strong that it was like a sledgehammer hitting the walls of fear the enemy had set up in my heart. Something big shifted, and something deep crumbled.

The next morning, I met with another friend, who offered to pray with me. In our prayer, she asked Jesus to illuminate the memories that he wanted to heal. Through that time of prayer, I came to understand with clarity the root lie that I had agreed with many years prior. I invited Jesus into those horrific memories with my brother and asked him to speak the truth. It's difficult to describe a supernatural experience because natural words can't quite express it; it's literally out of this world. In essence, Jesus spoke the truth deeply and directly into the lie that I had believed for most of my life. He told me that he was there in my bedroom with me the whole time, that he was protecting me from greater harm, and that the power the enemy had was never and never will come close to his power.

The enemy is not more powerful
than God.

This reality blew the doors off my small, distorted understanding of God and opened up a deep place of hope in my heart. New hope emerged that the power of God, who truly has won the battle against the enemy, and who raised Jesus from the dead, was living in me! I was able to break the agreement I had made with the enemy's lies by rejecting the lie and making a new agreement with the Truth. From that moment on, the horrible memories from my past lost their grip of fear on me.

I could see Jesus in my past, standing right beside me in my most terrifying memories.

Along with the healing of my memories, I also experienced healing from all of my physical pain, anxiety, and dizziness.

Healing the root truly does bear good fruit.

Today, I am still experiencing the good and lasting fruit from that healing encounter with Jesus. Along with the physical and spiritual healing, there has been an ongoing restoration and healing of the relationship with my brother. I was able to let go of my resentment and forgive him, and I now consider him a very dear friend. He has become a wonderful presence in our family and brings us all so much joy. Over the years, we have been able to talk about different parts of our painful past, a past that he couldn't even remember due to the oppression he was living under. When he listened to my story and what he had put me through, he apologized immediately. He didn't even hesitate to acknowledge how terrible it must have been for me and how deeply sorry he was for everything. Through the healing work in my own life, Christ is healing my brother too.

"What may seem impossible, is possible for God" (Lk 1:7).

Sometimes when we hear a testimony of healing, we can get the impression that it seems incredibly fast and easy, but the reality is that it wasn't. It took me years of living in the pain of self-reliance to be brought to the point of hitting rock bottom, of crying out to God each day, and finally experiencing

breakthrough. One of the many things I learned was to hang on
in the midst of suffering, even when all seems lost. The truth is

---

we never know when a breakthrough is
right around the corner.

Healing can be instant, but often it's a journey. Where many of
us desire immediate healing, God desires intimacy, relationship,
and deep abiding love.

Healing is always about intimacy, not
just the removal of pain.

Whether we have realized it or not, we all have an enemy.
He is the devil, who wants to deceive us into believing God is
not for us, that he is not good or trustworthy, and that he is
withholding good things from us. John 8:44 teaches us that the
enemy is "a murderer from the beginning, not holding to the
truth, for there is no truth in him. When he lies, he speaks his
native language, for he is a liar and the father of lies." He will lie
to us about everything so that distrust, pride, and fear will take
root in our hearts and cause a rupture in our union with God.

These roots bear bad fruit in our lives, and sinful behavior
is a significant part of that. As we come to believe there is an
enemy at work in the world and in our lives, we can fall into
a trap of believing he is as powerful as God. We can become
disoriented by viewing God and the devil as equals in power
and anxiously wonder who is going to win the battle. The truth
is that God has already won the battle against the enemy. The
Catechism of the Catholic Church tells us, "Victory over the
'prince of this world' was won once for all at the Hour when

Jesus freely gave himself up to death to give us his life. This is the judgment of this world, and the prince of this world is 'cast out'" (2853).

Jesus has already won the battle, and we learn from scripture that through our Baptism the power of Jesus is at work in us; we are not powerless against the lies of the enemy!

> Finally, be strong in the Lord and in his mighty power. Put on the full armor of God, so that you can take your stand against the devil's schemes. For our struggle is not against flesh and blood, but against the rulers, against the authorities, against the powers of this dark world, and against the spiritual forces of evil in the heavenly realms. Therefore, put on the full armor of God, so that when the day of evil comes, you may be able to stand your ground, and after you have done everything, to stand. Stand firm then, with the belt of truth buckled around your waist, with the breastplate of righteousness in place, and with your feet fitted with the readiness that comes from the gospel of peace. In addition to all this, take up the shield of faith, with which you can extinguish all the flaming arrows of the evil one. Take the helmet of salvation and the sword of the Spirit, which is the word of God. (Eph 6:10–17)

Here, God is teaching us that although we have an enemy that is not flesh and blood, he has given us his power and spiritual weapons to stand firm against the enemy.

As I described in the last chapter, each of us has moments in our stories when pain and tragedy hit us. We might be tempted to compare our pain with someone else's and feel that our experience is insignificant, but minimizing our pain by comparing it with the pain of others only becomes a stumbling block to opening to healing and keeps us believing that coping is the best option. Every life and experience is unique. *Your hurts and*

wounds matter. They are not insignificant and cannot be compared to what someone else may have gone through. Maybe you
suffered physical or emotional abuse from a family member,
or perhaps a teacher, friend, or community member spoke lies
into your identity. Possibly betrayal and loneliness have reached
your doorstep. Or did living under harsh expectations and reactions from a parent make you feel you have to work hard in
order to be loved? Again, regardless of your story and wounds,
they matter. You matter to God and so does every detail of your
life. He desires for us to live life to the fullest, not live a life full
of hopeless coping. On the other hand, we can make our pain
an idol by giving it so much focus that we remain perpetually
a victim. This is not the answer either. "For freedom, Christ set
us free" (Gal 5:1).

The enemy wants to take whatever pain you have experienced and exploit it in any way he can so you will doubt the
heart of God and distance yourself from him. At the same time,
God desires to take every pain, suffering, disappointment,
heartache, and loss and bring healing, wholeness, and beauty
out of it. How do we know this? Because this is what he did
with the Cross. He experienced the worst possible suffering
and pain, but through his death and resurrection, he defeated
death, won eternal life for us, and made a way for us to be with
him in heaven forever. The crucifix was once a sign of shame
and horror but now has become the sign of the greatest act of
love the world will ever know, a sign of beauty and hope. The
way of the Cross is not a story that ends in death. It is a reality
that, when walked completely, ends in new life. *Good Friday
is not good without Easter Sunday.* Each of us is being invited
by Jesus to walk with him through the Paschal Mystery, from
suffering to death to new life.

A Practical Tool

It can feel daunting to look at our whole life and understand where we have made agreements with the lies of the enemy, where we need God to speak the truth, what the negative fruit is, and how to experience restoration. We need to grow in self-knowledge, which is an important spiritual discipline that takes practice. St. Teresa of Avila says, "Self-knowledge is so important that, even if you were raised right up to the heavens, I should like you never to relax your cultivation of it."[1]

One tool I have found helpful in the process of self-knowledge is to break down your life into smaller sections. This makes it easier to access memories and see our experiences with greater clarity. It's like sectioning off your house into separate rooms. I created a chart to assist you in the process, but feel free to make your own if you need more room. Take some time to write down the stages of your life in five- or ten-year sections, whatever seems most suitable for your age. Go back into each stage and write what you remember. Ask yourself, what are the two or three most prominent positive and negative messages I received in that time frame? Then ask yourself, what are the beliefs I have from each of those messages? Which beliefs are lies? What truth does Jesus want to speak into that lie? Finally, invite Jesus to come into each message with his truth.

LIFE MESSAGES

Write down the memories and messages from your story
in chronological order.

AGE	MEMORIES	POSITIVE MESSAGES	NEGATIVE MESSAGES
0 – 5			
6 – 11			
12 – 17			
18 – 23			
24 – 29			
30 – 35			

WHAT IS THE TRUTH THAT JESUS WANTS ME TO KNOW?

LIFE MESSAGES

Write down the memories and messages from your story
in chronological order.

AGE	MEMORIES	POSITIVE MESSAGES	NEGATIVE MESSAGES
0 – 10			
11 – 21			
22 – 32			
33 – 43			
44 – 54			
55 – 65			

WHAT IS THE TRUTH THAT JESUS WANTS ME TO KNOW?

Chapter 4

BLOCKS TO HEALING

One beautiful morning, my husband and I set out on an adventure with three other couples who are some of our dearest friends. We were all so excited to be together and experience the beauty of British Columbia together. The majesty of the enormous mountains, the water, and the evergreens are hard to beat. We had a leisurely trip planned to canoe from the beach of a local lake and down a winding river, stop for a picnic lunch along the water's edge, and finish up by a lovely golf course where we would be picked up and taken to a beautiful dinner that would be prepared for us. The day was supposed to be peaceful and fun. It started with sunshine, laughter, splashing each other, and taking in the scenery, but soon, it turned into something none of us expected.

Within the first hour, the winds picked up and were headed directly toward us with such force that although we were rowing with all our might, we barely moved in the water. What was supposed to take about three hours was going to take us all day. As we struggled to paddle, we noticed the water had risen so dramatically in the weeks prior to our trip that there was no longer a beach to stop along to take breaks or have lunch. The river's edge had disappeared, and the water had risen so high that the sides were met with sheer rock cliffs and trees.

As we pressed on, the weather continued to turn, the clouds began to look stormy, and soon the water was splashing into the boat as the bow thumped loudly against the waves. There wasn't one other person on the water other than us. Fear gripped us as we endured hours of strenuous paddling and being whipped into the middle of the river by opposing currents that caused whirlpools. Jake and I kicked into survival mode and did everything we could to make it to the end as fast as possible.

That day didn't turn out as expected because there were so many blocks we didn't expect along the journey. We weren't prepared enough, nor did we have the tools to navigate them properly. The good news is we survived and lessons were learned. The next time we go on a canoe trip we will know how to navigate the journey a lot more smoothly because when we understand what blocks we might face, we know how to prepare, deal with them, or avoid them.

There are so many blocks in the journey of healing that an entire book could be written on that topic alone, but there are a few I'd like to focus on that I think are some of the most common and significant. I have already touched on some of them in previous chapters, such as minimizing the pain in our story and the role of the enemy, but in this chapter, I would like to talk about practical atheism, unforgiveness, sin, and self-reliance, and expand on the power that lies and agreements have. I believe that if we are able to understand and name the blocks we struggle with, we are more likely to be able to do the work to remove them with God's help. Blocks are not permanent; they can be moved, broken down, and the pathway made clear. Jesus can always make a way.

Practical Atheism

I have a dear friend who grew up in a very broken family environment. One of her parents had mental illness, and the other just didn't engage very much. She often had to fend for herself and had deep pain from being left alone and her needs not being met. As an adult, she has been working in full-time Church ministry for more than twenty years. She faithfully attends Mass and receives the sacraments; she has an active prayer life and has deliberately chosen to give her life to Jesus.

Here's the thing: Although all of this is true, my friend has a deep belief about God that bubbles up to the surface every time life gets hard, or things don't go right. The experience of hardship seems to negate most of the goodness, truth, and beauty that she "knows" about God when times are good and draws her into a place of orphan living where she feels alone, abandoned, Fatherless, and reliant on herself to get through. This is a pattern of lies, false beliefs, and unhealthy responses that seem to play out for her when life challenges. It seems she suddenly becomes more of an atheist in her mind and her actions—as if she doesn't have a loving Father in heaven who desires her good—rather than a faith-filled Catholic. I actually think this type of practical atheism, where we live and act as if the promise of the Gospel doesn't exist and we are on our own, isn't unique to my friend; rather, it is extremely common among all of us who identify as "believers."

We are meant to live through each day and circumstance with the knowledge that our identity is as sons and daughters of a loving Father, that everything he has is our inheritance, and that the resurrection power that raised Christ Jesus from the dead is living in us, but this is a huge challenge for most of us. Hardships occur, and instead of living out of that security in our identity and love of the Father, we live in practical ways as atheists. Our faith seems to quickly disintegrate, and we operate as if we are on our own, an orphan without a heavenly Father who will provide, thus being no different than one who doesn't believe in God. This might be a pattern of thinking and living, but it doesn't have to stay that way.

When we do live in the security and knowledge of being beloved children of God, we believe that even when life is hard, really hard, we are in the palm of God's hand and are being taken care of by him. The truth is that "in all these things we are more than conquerors through him who loved us. For I am convinced that neither death, nor life, nor angels, nor rulers, nor things present, nor things to come, nor powers, nor height, nor depth, nor anything else in all creation, will be able to separate us from the love of God in Christ Jesus our Lord" (Rom 8:37–39). When life does deal us pain, we can pray for the gift of faith and pray that instead of living as an orphan, we will lean into Jesus as our life, hope, and provider for all that we need.

Unforgiveness

God is a God of love, and we were made in his image. We will become most alive and who we were designed to be when we mirror our Creator and live as people of love and mercy. It sounds easy in concept but in practice is an area where we have an enormous amount of trouble with the follow-through. We allow ourselves to be duped into thinking that not forgiving the people who have hurt us is easier than the process of forgiveness, but I think it's because we underestimate the power and negative consequences of unforgiveness in our lives. Even on a physical level, research shows that unforgiveness can dramatically affect a person's physical health. An article from Johns Hopkins says that unforgiveness "puts you into a fight-or-flight mode, which results in numerous changes in heart rate, blood pressure, and immune response. Those changes, then, increase the risk of depression, heart disease, and diabetes, among other conditions. Forgiveness, however, calms stress levels, leading to improved health."[1] Unforgiveness is bad for our health, but more important, it's also bad for our souls and relationships and blocks the movement of the Holy Spirit to heal, restore, and set free.

Unforgiveness inhibits hurt relationships from ever healing while also keeping us bound to the past. This makes us incapable of embracing the "future full of hope" that the Lord has planned for us (Jer 29:11). God wants us to abide in his love, and to do this he asks that we would forgive others with the same level of mercy that God has extended to us. "Let all bitterness and wrath and anger and clamor and slander be put away from you, with all malice, and be kind to one another, tenderhearted, forgiving one another, as God in Christ forgave you" (Eph 4:31–32). Christ died for us when we were still sinners (see Romans 5:8); he didn't wait for us to change, and he didn't even wait for us to say we are sorry. He chose to love and forgive when it was totally undeserved and didn't make sense from a human perspective.

There are so many reasons we tell ourselves that we can't or shouldn't forgive. We all have people that have hurt us so deeply. Maybe they abused us or someone we love, lied, stole, cheated, were unfaithful, abandoned us, gossiped, ruined our reputation, treated us with hate, or were racist, bigoted, judgmental, cold, angry, distant, hateful, or absent. Or maybe we were that person who caused the hurt and we can't forgive ourselves. We can easily convince ourselves that if we don't forgive someone, it's the last thing that keeps them accountable or causes them some pain, when in reality it's more like what Malachy McCourt said: "Resentment is like taking poison and waiting for the other person to die."[2]

Ultimately, we end up hurting ourselves more when we choose not to forgive because it keeps us stuck in the moment of the hurt and blocks the future of freedom that God desires for us.

In a way, it binds us to the wound and the memory of when it happened, so we aren't able to let go, move on, or heal. God desires our freedom, and he doesn't expect us to do it all on our own. Mercy is an extension of the heart of God and a gift we need to ask God to give to us, for ourselves, and to offer to others. When something is impossible for us, it is not impossible for God and the riches of his mercy are there for us to access at any time. A place to start might be to bring your unforgiveness and pain to the Sacrament of Reconciliation, also known as a sacrament of healing. It's not just where we confess our sins but also a place where the floodgates of God's power, mercy, healing, strength, and grace are poured into our hearts so we can live in the freedom we were meant for.

Forgiveness doesn't mean we have to trust the person again; they may not be worthy of trust. It doesn't mean we can't have boundaries or that we open ourselves up to abusive behavior; some relationships need strong boundaries and sometimes healthy distance. It does mean, however, that even when things aren't going to look perfect, we can still access the mercy and grace of God to choose forgiveness and let go of resentment by placing it into the hands of Jesus. It also doesn't mean that we will be able to forget, but we can experience healing of our memories, a shift in our perspective, and a knowledge of God's presence in the wound so our memories don't haunt and continue to traumatize us. Forgiveness opens doors to our own healing in powerful ways.

Sin

We have just discussed various ways people have sinned against us, but we also need to acknowledge that a huge block to healing and our relationship with God is our own sin. Scripture tells us that "all have sinned and fall short of the glory of God"

(Rom 3:23). It also tells us to "live as free men, but do not use your freedom to cover up for evil; live as servants of God" (1 Pt 2:16). We all know we suffer as a result of the fall of Adam and Eve, and as much as we would like to say, "Well, I didn't choose that in the garden, so why do I have to suffer from it?" we do choose to sin each and every day of our lives. It's hard to face our shortcomings and be honest about our attachments to things that lead us away from God instead of toward God, but getting real and honest is a big part of being healed. For deep and lasting healing to occur,

---

the secrets have to come out of the
darkness and into the light.

In Alcoholics Anonymous they have a saying—"you are only as sick as your secrets"—and I believe this is very true. The more secrets we have, the more shame and sin can fester there, but when we bring them into the light, they lose their power and no longer have the same hold on us.

Lord of the Rings is one of the most epic stories of a battle between the light and the dark.[3] You can't help but see the Catholic elements of J. R. R. Tolkien's faith come through in his writing of this amazing trilogy. I particularly love the movie scene in *Lord of the Rings: The Two Towers* where the good King Théoden has been placed under the spell and lies of his enemy.[4] He is withering away and has lost his kingly authority and power under the spell. Gandalf, the wizard and Christ figure in the story, enters King Théoden's chamber and says to him, "Too long have you sat in the shadows." He raises his staff, calls the king's name, reminds him of his royal lineage, and breaks the spell. King Théoden is immediately set free from the oppressive spell and restored back to himself.

We have all sat in the shadows for far too long; we have fallen under the oppression of darkness within our hearts and made decisions to turn away from God. We have allowed sin to enter into our lives and create distance from the One who loves us and desires our greatest good. God is not mad at us; he wants us to be satisfied, so he has given us desires that can only be fulfilled by him. When we allow a desire for something good to be directed at something else for our own selfish pleasures, we will ultimately be left unsatisfied. We see this all throughout the scriptures and in the lives of each human being, but we also see conversion can happen. We can choose to turn away from the darkness and step into the light.

> This is the message we have heard from him and proclaim to you, that God is light and in him, there is no darkness at all. If we say that we have fellowship with him while we are walking in darkness, we lie and do not do what is true; but if we walk in the light as he himself is in the light, we have fellowship with one another, and the blood of Jesus his Son cleanses us from all sin. (1 Jn 1:5–7)

God is all things that are good, true, and beautiful. When we mortally sin, it blocks charity, severs our relationship with God, and breaks our covenant with God. When we go to the Sacrament of Reconciliation, our relationship with God and the Church is restored. We need to run to this sacrament frequently, to bring the darkness into the light and receive the grace we need to root out sin in our life. We are all carrying around the weight of our sin. Addiction, pride, unforgiveness, gluttony, lust, and perfectionism—there is an endless list of ways we are far away from God and desperately need the resurrection power of Jesus. Jesus is the only way. There aren't three easy steps to solve our problems, but there is a person, Jesus, who can understand our pain and who has the power to heal and forgive. Each of us has a choice to make. Will we die to our sin, experience healing, and live a new life abiding in Christ? It is also important to ask ourselves, why are we choosing to sin in the particular ways we do? What is the desire that is at the root of our misguided attempts to satisfy ourselves? What is the lie that we believe about why God can't satisfy that desire?

We are not meant to live a double life;
we are meant to live the full life in the
freedom of Christ who has shattered
the chains of darkness.

Self-Reliance

In all of the healing work I have personally done over the years, and in accompanying other people in their own healing, one of the most prominent blocks to healing is self-reliance. It's the opposite of abiding in Jesus and surrendering to him. We are not meant to live life alone, yet for many of us, we don't know how to do it any other way. A shift needs to be made within our minds and our hearts away from believing we have to take care of it ourselves, or even that we are capable of doing it on our own, and move toward dependency on Jesus. Jesus clearly says to us in Matthew 18:3, "Truly I tell you, unless you change and become like children, you will never enter the kingdom of heaven." If there's one thing I've learned from being a parent, it's that little children are totally dependent on parents for everything. If you don't feed them, change them, soothe them, and cuddle them, they will die. Literally, their lives depend on you.

Jesus is showing us that we are always supposed to live as children, and in the places we have turned to independence, we need to become dependent on him once again. After all the ups and downs, successes and failures, in my forty-four years of life, I have never believed this more than I do now: the way to heaven is through littleness and surrender. I used to have such a tight grip on my life and all the things around me. I believed it was all up to me, but the weight of it crushed me. The times I have felt most free and at ease are when I gave up my false sense of control and lay down in the capable arms of Jesus. There is so much comfort and peace that comes from the knowledge that it's not all up to me, that I don't have to do it all or figure it all out, that

---

it's okay to be weak because I have a faithful, strong Father who is with me and will not let me go.

He will work all things for good, *all things*, because I love him and am daily giving it to him and opening myself up to his provision (see Romans 8:28). If we truly want to abide in the love of God, as Jesus talks about in John 15, then we need to let go of our control and open wide the door to Jesus being the Lord of our lives.

Lies and Agreements

Lies and agreements are extremely powerful in our lives. As I described in my own story, when we're hurt and bad things happen to us, it's fertile ground for the enemy to lie to us and create a narrative that pulls us away from our relationship with God and others. It's as if he is throwing negative lies like seeds into the soil of our heart, mind, and body. What makes those seeds take root, grow, and eventually bear bad fruit in our life is our agreement with those lies. When the enemy lies to us, we have a decision to make: either we reject the lie or we agree with it and believe it as if it were the truth.

All of us have lies we have agreed with that have taken root within us. Right now, we believe those are true. The painful situations are unique to each of us, but the lies and our agreements are often similar. They can often sound like these types of beliefs: I am a disappointment, I am not worthy of love, I'm too much, I'm not enough, I'm not loveable, I'm a loser, I'm a failure, I don't measure up, I don't have what it takes, I'm weak, I'm ugly, I'm unwanted, everyone will abandon me, I will always be alone, I have to be productive to be valuable, I have to fake it so I will be accepted, I'm dirty, people will always let me down, I can't trust anyone, I am unforgivable, I will never be happy, and it will never get better. There are so many more, and maybe they are coming to mind right now as you read this.

There is hope, friends. All is not lost to the lies that are raging with us, planted by the enemy. Jesus wants to speak his truth and give us the opportunity to reject the lies and agree with his truth. When we do that, truth can take root in place of the lie and bear beautiful fruit. We need our minds to be transformed with the truth and that will lead us into freedom and transformed lives.

The movie *The Hunger Games* is a story about a hierarchy within a society, the most popular of which creates a game for their own entertainment, where the contestants from the lower class have to fight to the death to win the game.[5] The lower class essentially lives as slaves under the rule of the upper class. There are two main characters, a young woman named Katniss and a young man named Peeta, who are friends who have known each other since they were children. Through the ups and downs of the story, they stay close and protect each other at every turn.

At one point in the story, Peeta gets kidnapped by the upper class. They isolate him from everyone and essentially brainwash him by implanting false memories in his mind until he believes the upper class is good and Katniss is the enemy. When he is released, he believes lies about Katniss being the enemy to the extent that he attempts to kill her several times. Katniss refuses to abandon Peeta and chooses to stay close to him. Over time she continues to tell him the truth until he starts to trust her. It eventually becomes clear to him that he has two opposing narratives in his head, the truth and the lie, but he doesn't always know how to distinguish them. He needs Katniss to help him know which is false and which isn't. He opens up to her about some of his memories, and at the end of each one he asks her if it's a real memory or not real.

Through his persistence in bringing out the lie and asking for the truth to be spoken, all of the lies are eventually exposed; he heals and is able to live in the truth. We need to know what the lies are so that we hear the voice of Truth and live in the freedom of the truth that we are beloved, chosen, seen, heard, valuable, enough, beautiful, worthy, and accepted. We need to know, deep in our bones, that the love of the Father can restore everything. I will speak more about how to practically do this later in the book.

As I said at the beginning of this chapter, blocks are not permanent; they can be moved and the pathway made clear.

At this point, you might be feeling overwhelmed and hearing the enemy whispering some discouraging words. I want to reassure you that this is a journey and is meant to be moved through little by little. When we look at a huge mountain it can seem daunting to climb it, but if we focus on one step at a time, we can eventually get to where we need to be. Thankfully, you are not alone; Jesus is here, and the communion of saints is at your side. It's vital to know you don't have to wait until you're healed to be close to Jesus because union with Jesus happens in the journey, while you're in the midst of the work. There are a lot of practical steps in this book and many more to come that will be like signposts along the path to help you navigate the healing journey.

Pause & REFLECT

Take some time to journal and reflect on the following questions:

What are some of the blocks to healing you can recognize in your life right now?

What are some of the key lies you believe about God and yourself?

Take a moment to ask God to give you the grace of forgiveness and healing. Ask him what truth he wants you to know about that relationship that is broken.

Take some time to study the chart on the next page and reflect on the qualities of God's voice versus Satan's voice.

DISCERNING THE VOICES

The voice we listen to impacts what we believe.

GOD'S VOICE	ENEMY'S VOICE
GIVES HOPE	CONDEMNS
MERCIFUL	BRINGS DESPAIR
GIVES PEACE	DISCOURAGES
CONVICTS	CREATES STRESS
STRENGTHENS	HARSH
COMFORTS	CAUSES WORRY
KIND	DECEIVES
TRUE	SHAMING
LOVING	LIES
REASSURES	ACCUSES
GUIDES	CONFUSES
PATIENT	CAUSES FEAR
GENTLE	ABUSES
RESTORES	CREATES CHAOS

MESSAGES I BELIEVE ABOUT MYSELF, GOD, AND OTHERS

In what areas of your life do you desire to hear God's voice?

In what areas of your life do you regularly hear Satan's voice speaking instead of God?

Chapter 5

THE PERSONALITY OF JESUS

Now that we have discussed the distinction between the voice of God and the voice of Satan, let's deepen our understanding of who the person of Jesus is so we can grow in our relationship with him. In this chapter, we will explore different scenes from scripture that depict the personality of Jesus. I'm going to begin by sharing with you the ways my children communicate, which prompted me to discover who Jesus is beyond the words he says in scripture.

My son is sarcastic and playful—his sarcasm isn't cutting; it's just funny. It's his unique quirks, tone, and glint of playfulness in his eye when he says these things that give me all the cues I need to know what he means. People who don't know him hear him say certain things and wonder if he's serious. They don't understand that 90 percent of what he says is playful. He also has a super tender heart and will say the most charming things that make me feel honored and loved as his mom. If I didn't know him well, I might wonder if he was just joking again, but because I do know him, I know the difference between him being sweet and being humorous without him having to explain.

My daughter, Eva, wears her heart on her sleeve. You always know what is on her mind because her face and body tell the story. Her eyes glimmer and her face lights up when she thinks of something wonderful. Even the way she holds her body tells me whether she's had a bad day or a great day. As human beings we communicate both verbally and nonverbally. Our nonverbals usually make up the majority of what we communicate to those around us. This is what is so beautiful about relationships: we get to know the interior movements of another person's heart and their unique expressions through their body.

Jesus wants us to know him in this same way—intimately and personally. He is God who took on human flesh, made with the same ability to communicate both verbally and nonverbally. The TV series called *The Chosen* has done a great job at opening a very human perspective on the personality of Jesus.[1] You hear the character of Jesus say words from scripture, but now you have facial expressions and tone of voice that we may not have perceived before. It changes everything. When you know someone so well, you notice all the nuances, a change in their breathing, a slight curve of their mouth, the way their eyebrows lift or furrow slightly, and you just know. No words, just a look, and you understand.

Have you ever wondered who Jesus really is? Of course, scripture tells us he is God, the faithful one, the Messiah, the Savior, the Teacher, the King of kings, and Emmanuel God with us, but have you ever wondered who he was as a man? What his personality was like? What it was like to hang out with him?

It's easy to confuse what we have heard about God with what it means to really know him in a personal way.

For many years, I was discovering a lot about God, theologically, but also what it meant to be in a relationship with him. I was learning to see God in the daily moments of my life, but it wasn't until I took a deeper look at the scriptures, with the intention of discovering his personality, that I came to a deeper understanding of who Jesus really is. This took my relationship with him to a significantly greater depth because as I discovered more about him, his heart, his kindness, and his character, I was captivated and fell in love with him all over again.

For many of us as Christians, we can confuse what we *do* in regard to our faith with a *relationship* with Jesus. Although it's wonderful to go to church, to read spiritual books, to practice spiritual disciplines, and to pray the Rosary and novenas, those things do not necessarily lead to a personal relationship with Jesus. They can just stay in the categories of good works, duty, or perhaps even obligation. Those things aren't bad, but they shouldn't be the goal. Remember, *the goal is union and intimacy.* It's not box-checking, to-do lists, performing, or striving. *Obligation will never result in a love affair.* The goal is abiding in intimacy with the Lover of our souls. So, let's open up a couple of scriptures and see what they show us about the personality of Jesus. As you read through these scriptures, I would encourage you to pause and try to picture the scene, even imagine yourself there, because these aren't just stories but real moments in history in which Jesus has chosen to communicate something about himself to us.

Jesus Raises the Widow's Son at Nain

> Soon afterwards he went to a town called Nain, and his disciples and a large crowd went with him. As he approached the gate of the town, a man who had died was being carried out. He was his mother's only son, and she was a widow; and with her was a large crowd from the town. When the Lord saw her, he had compassion for her and said to her, "Do not weep." Then he came forward and touched the bier, and the bearers stood still. And he said, "Young man, I say to you, rise!" The dead man sat up and began to speak, and Jesus gave him to his mother. (Lk 7:11–15)

Oh, the kindness of Jesus. Let's set the scene. Prior to this moment, Jesus has been traveling around with his disciples and a growing group of followers. He has been preaching revolutionary messages, he has been working miracles, and there is quite a buzz around him. I mean, could you imagine seeing someone healing the blind and the sick? Wouldn't you want to see what would happen next?

He enters the town of Nain with a huge group of followers and comes into the middle of a funeral procession. The mother has already suffered the death of her husband and has now lost her son, so she likely has lost everything, including any social status in a world where a woman's place was determined in reference to the men in her life. Little does she know that her life and identity are about to be determined by this new man, Jesus, in the most profound way. She is weeping as she experiences the agony of another precious life lost in her family.

In the midst of this loud and chaotic environment, Jesus is so attuned to her. Instead of being distracted by all the people or finding his identity in being the celebrity, he notices her crying and walks right up to her and says, "Don't cry." The tenderness of those words and of his voice at that moment! He notices her, he sees her pain, and he is drawn right to her with compassion. I could imagine as he tells her not to cry that he gently places his hand on the side of her face and carefully wipes her tears away with his thumb. His eyes, full of love, are locked with hers. I wonder if she sensed something at that moment if his words were both compassionate and compelling. Did he also have a glint of joy flash in his eyes as he thought about what he was about to do next?

In those days, touching a dead body was considered unclean, but Jesus was not concerned with the law or people's impressions; rather, he was concerned with the heart and the people who were hurting. He walked right up to the dead young man and placed his hands on him. Getting close wasn't enough; he wanted to touch the dead with his hands, which reveals to us that Jesus is not afraid of death, of the stench, of the ugliness, and of the seemingly impossible situation. It also shows us that

---

Jesus isn't repulsed by the places in us that are sinful, ugly, messy, full of depravity, the dark rooms in our hearts, our gaping wounds, or the dead places within.

He isn't repulsed; he is drawn to them because he loves us and he has the power to heal it, "for nothing will be impossible with God" (Lk 1:37).

The Call and Restoration of Peter

One of my favorite relationships in scripture that reveals the heart of God for us is between Jesus and Peter. Peter was just a guy, a fisherman whom many see as a bit brash and rough around the edges, but he loved Jesus and had the courage to be one of the first to leave everything behind. Can we just imagine that scene for a moment? Scripture says, "Jesus was walking by the Sea of Galilee. He saw two brothers. They were Simon (his other name was Peter) and Andrew, his brother. They were putting a net into the sea for they were fishermen. Jesus said to them, "Follow Me. I will make you fish for men!" At once they left their nets and followed Him" (Mt 4:18–20).

Peter is out fishing and meets Jesus, who invites Peter to follow him . . . and Peter does. We usually gloss over that, as if that would be totally normal, but it's far from normal. Sometimes we need to visualize scripture in a current situation to make it more real. Imagine that you are at work at your local coffee shop. It's just a normal day with your coworkers, and people are coming and going all around you. Then a man gets in line, and instead of ordering a coffee he looks into your eyes and says, "Follow me." Who would say yes to that? Most of us would look at him with total confusion, possibly let out a small laugh, and then maybe call the cops on the crazy man. But this was not Peter's response, so something was different about this man. What was it? What would the look in his eyes and the tone of his voice have to be that you would drop your little barista apron and walk out the door with him? Not just walk out the door but *follow* him and in the process willingly leave your friends and your entire family behind?

There must have been something in his eyes when he looked at Peter that made Peter trust him.

Jesus must have been so compelling.

He must have been like no one else, exuding something that made Peter instantly believe that he had something he desperately wanted. I imagine a mix of captivating love, wild adventure, safety, and a feeling of being known. He must have been so good, in fact, that Peter would be willing to leave behind his beloved wife and everything in his life to follow this man. Now that makes me fascinated and curious about Jesus.

Another thing I can see in the character and personality of God through Peter's story is that God is unfailing both in his love and in his desire for us.

He chooses us for kingdom purposes, and he has plans for us, even though we will fail him. God is faithful in his love, even when we lose our way.

We always have a place in his family, and he always has a plan beyond what we are worthy of. We know that although Peter was a friend and follower of Jesus, Peter would betray him. Before it ever happened, Jesus knew it would, and still, he chose Peter and kept choosing Peter even after Peter betrayed him.

I've been betrayed by friends. I've experienced them abandoning me and saying hurtful things, and it's absolutely devastating. Although I've been able to move on and in some cases reestablish a relationship, I don't exactly want to trust them again, never mind entrust one of the most important things in the world to them. But Jesus is not like us. His love is steady, faithful, and total, even though we are continually unfaithful to him. There are no conditions for us to be faithful, for him to love us and choose us. We see this in an incredible way in the life of Peter and particularly the care Jesus has for him in his failure.

I can imagine the moment that Peter was standing by that charcoal fire after denying Jesus three times and the rooster crowed. Jesus was passing by at that time, and they locked eyes. There was no hiding what had just happened, and it was the very thing that Peter promised he would never do. Oh, the pain and the shame that Peter must have felt. I can imagine the horrible feeling of dread tingling through his body, the color draining out of his face, and the hot tears that must have welled up in his eyes and begun to slowly fall down his cheeks. Within moments he ran away and wept.

Those eyes. The same eyes that had captivated Peter when Jesus said, "Follow me," looked at him in the exact moment of his sin and betrayal, and were still filled with love. Jesus could see all of Peter, and he loved him and Peter knew it. There was no time for Peter to apologize or make amends because shortly after that Jesus was beaten, stripped, mocked, crucified, and then died. He hung on that Cross, abandoned, humiliated, betrayed, for the sins and infidelity of Peter, and you and me.

Peter, who was at a complete loss and overwhelmed with shame, went back to what he knew, which was fishing. He was on the boat, with his clothes stripped off, when he heard a familiar voice calling from the shore asking if he had caught any fish. It was Jesus. Jesus must have had a twinkle in his eye and a smirk on his face. He had used these words before, but this time he had just risen from the dead, defeated death, and made a way for us to be with him forever in heaven. He must have been ecstatic! He showed up on that beach not to condemn but to restore Peter's heart. Jesus is waiting to restore our hearts too.

In an instant Peter knew it was Jesus. The scriptures say that because he was naked, Peter put his robe on and jumped in the water. I always wondered why he put his robe on when he was about to swim. As I prayed into that one day, I realized that this sounded so similar to Adam and Eve after their infidelity in Genesis 3:9 where Adam said, "I was naked so I hid." It made me wonder if Peter put his clothes on to hide the shame of his nakedness, to cover up the shame of his unfaithful heart, to hide his vulnerability out of fear. Scripture says Peter swam to the shore, but we don't know exactly what happened in this exchange. I can imagine, in my own encounter with the loving heart of God, that Jesus probably didn't wait for Peter to make it all the way to the shore, but like the prodigal father who ran to meet his son, I think Jesus ran into the water to meet Peter. I think he would have embraced him and kissed him, and I bet Peter just wept tears of repentance in his arms.

The kindness, depth, and attentiveness of Jesus are seen in that he had already built a fire for Peter and proceeded to make him breakfast. Peter must have been starving and cold after his swim from the boat, so Jesus has already anticipated his needs and provided for him. It's also powerful to note that this fire, just like the one that Peter stood in front of when he denied Jesus, was a charcoal fire. These are the only two charcoal fires mentioned in scripture. Jesus, in a small way, re-creates the scene of the betrayal and gives Peter the opportunity to not only reconcile and repent by affirming his love for Jesus but also experience healing of his memories and of that awful moment. Jesus could have embarrassed Peter, rubbed his nose in it, yelled at him, and made him feel like an utter failure, but he didn't and wouldn't. Jesus isn't like us; he is pure self-giving love. Jesus is here for Peter, not for himself.

There are so many more parts of the personality of Jesus that can be found in the scriptures and most importantly that we can come to discover and know right now because Jesus isn't a figure in history. He is alive and well. He has a body, he has a face; he is a real person who desires a relationship with us right now. He has compelling eyes that we will all look into one day, and those eyes are already gazing upon each of us. He has a real, human body that we will get to hug, real hands we will hold, and an audible voice we will hear. He has a smile, he has a laugh; he has a heart that is beating and overflowing with love for you and for me.

This chapter doesn't even skim the surface of who Jesus really is.

> The beautiful adventure of the Christian life is that we are invited into a personal relationship with this man, who is also the Creator of the universe, and he wants us to know him and fall in love with him—to abide in him.

As we grow in this relationship and discover the beauty of who he is, we will come to distinguish his voice from all the other voices; we will come to understand his calling on our lives and his will for us.

False Images of God

For many of us, we haven't seen or known Jesus in this way because we have most often experienced a false image of him. We might see him as a judge who wants to punish us, Santa Claus who shows up occasionally to give us gifts, a police officer who is waiting to get us in trouble for a mistake, or even a distant father. Unfortunately for most of us, we picked up these false impressions of who we think God is from the most influential adults in our early life. The wounding interactions with our parents or our primary caregiver, teachers, pastors, coaches, and other trusted adults, as well as the things we observed in them at a young age, were the filter through which we viewed God. If our parents were loving, we have likely had an easier time seeing God as loving, but if they were distant or angry, we have likely struggled to see God for the loving father he is.

I have an older friend in my life who has never really experienced the love of God in a personal way. There are several reasons for this, but the main one is because of the brokenness and pain she had experienced from her own earthly father. Her father was a very angry, abusive, and self-absorbed man. Along with growing up malnourished and in poverty, she was forced by her father to start working and miss school when she was just a child. Her father's words were harsh and cutting, and he would often say things like "you will never amount to anything" and "you are worthless." He was physically, emotionally, and sexually abusive, and this had a deep effect on not only her life but also her relationship with God. She has struggled with feeling she has to prove herself and earn love, she has an insatiable desire to be affirmed, and to this day she still believes more lies about herself, God, and others than she believes the truth.

Whether we realize it or not, our parents and caregivers have a dramatic impact on how we view God, what we believe about him, and our relationship with him.

Parents are the first lens that we see God through, and their wounds and gifts are a primary way we come to know or misunderstand who God is.

By calling God "Father," the language of faith indicates two main things: that God is the first origin of everything and transcendent authority; and that he is at the same time goodness and loving care for all his children. . . . The language of faith thus draws on the human experience of *parents, who are in a way the first representatives of God for man.* But this experience also tells us that *human parents are fallible and can disfigure the face of fatherhood and motherhood . . . no one is father as God is Father.* (*CCC*, 239; emphasis mine)

When we look back at our history, in light of this truth, we are able to uncover where some of our false views of God have their roots, which also provides the opportunity to experience healing and an encounter with who God really is.

God wants to reveal himself to us in every way he can: through his word, nature, beauty, and other people. In his kindness, God will send people into our lives to show us a part of who he is. My husband Jake calls this the mosaic of the face of God. When we open our hearts to the way God wants to restore our vision of him, we begin to encounter the real him. You might encounter a teacher who is patient, someone else's father who is gentle and kind, a coach who is encouraging and motivating, a spouse who knows how to love with purity and sincerity, or a mentor whom you know sees your value and gifts. All of these experiences can be moments of grace and healing.

Pause & REFLECT

Take some time to journal and reflect on the following questions:

Open your Bible and read the passage from the Gospel of John 3:1–2. Try to imagine the scene and imagine yourself there. What does this scripture show you about the personality and character of Jesus?

What are two positive ways your parents or primary caregivers reflected the face of God?

What are two negative ways your parents of primary caregivers disfigured the face of God?

Who are the people God has provided in your life that have reflected parts of his character and created a mosaic of his face?

Chapter 6

JESUS THE WAY

As we grow in our relationship with Jesus and seek to know him more intimately, it's important to pay attention to how he has chosen to reveal himself to us in scripture. In John 14:6, Jesus says, "I am the way and the truth and the life." In the next three chapters I will take us through some practical ways we can access and come to know personally Jesus the Way, Jesus the Truth, and Jesus the Life.

My husband, Jake, and I met during our first year at Franciscan University of Steubenville, Ohio. He had just transferred up from Auburn University, and I had just moved after serving for four years on a traveling evangelization team. We grew a friendship over a few months and soon decided to start dating. Seven months later we were engaged, and eight months after that we were married. I was twenty-four, he was twenty-three, and it was a beautiful time in our life. We were both committed to our faith, each invested in a personal relationship with God; we were studying theology and wanted to serve in the Church as our life mission, we had a great community of faith-filled friends, and we had even addressed some of the main struggles in our personal lives. I remember the fun and ease of those first two years of marriage. We went on lots of dates, watched movies at the theater, had lovely dinners out, played cards with friends, went on road trips, laughed a lot, and experienced all of our first memories as a married couple. Within two years we had a new beautiful baby girl and were living in our first real house in Denver, Colorado.

One afternoon we were talking and he was telling me how he had helped a friend who was struggling with pornography use and had encouraged him to go to a priest who was really good at counseling in that area. Something in my gut felt wrong, and I hesitantly asked, "How do you know the priest is good at that?" There was a long pause, and Jake glanced down. A sinking feeling filled my whole body as I waited for him to answer. As a result of significant childhood wounds and exposure at a young age, I knew Jake had struggled with pornography use in the past, but he had assured me he had worked through it and that it was no longer an issue.

There were moments in those first two years that I felt something wasn't right, but I was too afraid to ask or had convinced myself I was just being insecure. The seconds ticked by, and it felt like an eternity as I waited for him to answer. He finally took a deep breath and confessed that he had not overcome his addiction to pornography and that he had been seriously struggling with viewing it the whole time we were married. It felt like the blood drained from my face, and my heart fell into my feet. I was shattered. Being lied to is always painful. Being lied to by a spouse, the one whom you should never have to hide anything from, the one with whom you are totally vulnerable, was devastating.

My mind was spinning with questions. What else had he lied about? What were all the implications of this addiction? Who was he really? Did I make the wrong decision in marrying him? Hot tears rolled down my cheeks as he stumbled through his admission of the truth. I remember laying on the couch all night with our new baby, crying for hours, asking God why he had allowed all of this to happen. I felt feelings of rejection, betrayal, fear, anger, bitterness, sadness, hopelessness, and deep pain. In the morning, I remember him walking down the stairs with his head hanging low in shame. At that moment the Holy Spirit hovered over my heart and filled me with the strength to say the hardest words I've ever had to say to Jake: "I just want you to know, I love you . . . and this is not the kind of marriage we are going to have."

> The last thing I felt in my heart was love for him, but I was choosing it that day along with the tiniest glimmer of hope that somehow there was a way through this.

In the following days, we shared our painful story with a couple of dear friends from our church community, who lovingly came alongside us with words of hope and encouragement, plus some practical steps for moving forward. Jake was invited to be radically honest about what he needed and what he needed to be taken away to begin to heal and break the addiction to pornography and lust. His commitment allowed me to not take the role of policing his behavior or enforcing rules—it was his choice and commitment to his own healing.

He quickly dove into counseling, mentoring, fasting, prayer, and participation in a healing retreat. He was choosing to fight this battle with all of his might. As he battled, I found myself completely unraveled, vulnerable, and suffering. My heart was beginning to close off to him; I was in so much pain that I wanted to protect myself from ever being hurt again. My solution to that was to distance myself and shut my heart down. I knew that wasn't the right answer, but it was all I knew how to do to protect myself and cope. If I wanted to open the door to healing and move forward with Jake, I needed to learn a new way.

One day I was in the church praying and weeping when I heard the Lord speak to me in my heart. I sensed him say, "Heather, do you want what you had with Jake back?" "No," I said, "because it wasn't real, and I don't want to live in a lie." The Lord asked, "Do you want something new?" "Yes," I whispered through my tears. Then the Lord said the most important thing to me, an essential key to the healing journey: "If you want a new life, the only way to find it is through the Cross. Heather, are you willing to die and let the new life I have in store for your marriage come?" Ugh, the wrenching in my heart was palpable. I wept as I prayed. I finally answered him,

---

"Yes, Lord . . . I will die with you."

In the following months and years, Jake and I dove into all the avenues we believed would nurture and cultivate restoration in our marriage and in our individual hearts. Yes, I said years, because this is the reality. Healing isn't usually fast.

The microwave doesn't produce
a feast.

The journey of healing produces a relationship with God and the exchange of hearts, which protects against a selfish utility. Through those years of healing, we labored and fought for our marriage through fasting, counseling, healing retreats, personal prayer, renewing our minds and thoughts, mentoring, dating again, radical honesty, choosing forgiveness and openness, spending time in the healing gaze of Jesus in eucharistic adoration, time with community, and frequenting the sacraments. We cried a lot, it hurt a lot, but little by little, God was restoring us.

We didn't do things perfectly and it was not easy, but God was with us and we were moving through the Paschal Mystery, from suffering and death, to real resurrection freedom. The day that Jake confessed his addiction to pornography was the last day that he fell into that sin, and twenty years later, we are still married and believing in the goodness of God.

God truly is a miracle-working God,
and don't let anyone try to convince
you otherwise. You never know when
a miracle and breakthrough is right
around the corner.

Jesus never promised that life would be easy. In fact, he said in John 16:33, "in this world you will have trouble. But take heart! I have overcome the world" and, in John 12:24, "Very truly, I tell you, unless a grain of wheat falls into the earth and dies, it remains just a single grain; but if it dies, it bears much fruit." This is why Jesus is our hope. We have a resurrected God who promises that he can bring life to the dead and provide a new way when there seems to be no way. He doesn't just talk about it; he actually rose from the dead to new life and tells us that "the Spirit of God, who raised Jesus from the dead, lives in you" (Rom 8:11). This means the power of Christ given to live a new life is right there within us, where the Holy Spirit dwells.

You have to be willing to die to be able to rise, and to rise you need the only One who has defeated death, Jesus.

The call of every Christian is to follow Jesus, as it says in Matthew 16:4: "Then Jesus told his disciples, 'If any want to become my followers, let them deny themselves and take up their cross and follow me.'" The thing we don't realize is that he actually means what he says in this scripture. Following Jesus isn't just about being a good person or going to Mass or saying our prayers; it's about picking up our crosses and *following* him, letting him lead. We also don't often realize that because Jesus didn't just perpetually carry his cross, we aren't supposed to either. So many Catholics I encounter will talk about carrying their cross and believe that suffering is what it means to follow Jesus. But friends, suffering isn't the only part of following Jesus, and it definitely is not the end; resurrection is! Suffering doesn't make sense at all without the promise of the resurrection. Jesus wouldn't call us to suffer without a reason; that is not the kind of God we have. He is good, he is the Way that leads to new life, he wants the best for us, and sometimes suffering is involved to get it.

And not only that, but we also boast in our sufferings, knowing that suffering produces endurance, and endurance produces character, and character produces hope, and hope does not disappoint us, because God's love has been poured into our hearts through the Holy Spirit that has been given to us. (Rom 5:3–5)

Many of us will unknowingly wander around in circles with our cross for years, complaining about how heavy it is, and don't realize that we have actually lost sight of Jesus because he isn't walking in a tiny circle of suffering. He is walking ahead, inviting us to follow him and carry our cross up a hill where we will lay down on it and be crucified and die . . . so that we can rise! There is momentum in the Christian life; it's in living the Paschal Mystery, which is the suffering, death, resurrection, and ascension of Jesus, over and over again.

The road of suffering and death might be a long one, but when you're following and abiding in Jesus there is always a resurrection at the end.

"There is no evil to be faced that Christ does not face with us. There is no enemy that Christ has not already conquered. There is no cross to bear that Christ has not already born for us, and does not now bear with us."[1]

There are so many places within us that are suffering, and we have two options of what to do about it. Either we cope with the suffering, try to self-medicate, and white-knuckle our way through life or we allow our suffering to turn into a death that is hidden in the mystery and power of Jesus, where we then rise with him. "The saying is sure: If we have died with him, we will also live with him" (2 Tm 2:11). This scripture isn't just referring to heaven, but I truly believe and know it to be true that God wants us to experience the power of the resurrection in our lives right now. Jesus wants to bring his resurrection power into the areas of our hearts that are cold, broken, lost, and dead, and that have a big tombstone in front of them. Christ wants to roll away the stone and say to us, "Arise my beloved and come" (Sg 2:10).

For many of us, the fear of interior suffering and death is often greater than our desire to be free and experience new life. This is really a trick from the enemy, where he deceives us into thinking that living in chains is easier than living as free. Would we rather experience some pain when the chains are being broken off and be free, or would we rather skip the pain and stay a slave in chains forever? When faced with that truth, we can find our footing again, that freedom comes at a cost but leads to new life, whereas staying in slavery will only lead to death.

The enemy will try to steal our hope, especially when we are in the midst of suffering. He wants us to believe we can never be free and we should doubt the heart of God. This can even come through the voice of friends. I remember speaking with a dear friend, who was a priest, and as I told him the whole story about Jake and me, he said, "Heather don't get your hopes up. Addiction like this doesn't just go away and it will likely continue to be a part of your marriage." I mean, it sounded practical and realistic. He could've been right, but inside I felt anger rise up as I fought to refrain from throwing my phone out my car window. I replied, "Don't tell me that. I refuse to believe that God can't heal it. He has the power to restore even this."

I truly believe this was a grace that the Holy Spirit was pouring into my heart at that very moment, the gift of hope. It was clear that even my friend had lost hope in the healing power of

Christ in his own life and thus was sharing his conclusion that we can't hope for miracles. As Jake eventually walked into the resurrection and healing of this addiction, it ended up opening a door for that same friend of mine to start his own healing journey and a renewal of his hope in Jesus.

It's amazing how God can turn the most painful things into a source of hope and healing for others. I think most of us don't believe Jesus can and wants to work miracles in our lives. Often, we either subconsciously think that Jesus lived two thousand years ago and that's when the miracles ended or we might have the faith to believe that he still can work miracles today but that he won't work miracles in us. That's not true! "Jesus is the same, yesterday, today, and forever" (Heb 13:8).

There is no other way to a new life that we so desperately desire except to go through the Cross. As Archbishop Fulton J. Sheen says, "Unless there is a Good Friday, there can be no Easter Sunday."[2] Jesus explicitly speaks of this and lives this, but most importantly, he promises that he will be with us as we walk this mysterious road. If we truly are disciples of Jesus, then we are invited to follow him through the way that he has shown. It says so clearly in the *Catechism of the Catholic Church*, "The Paschal mystery has two aspects: by his death, Christ liberates us from sin; by his Resurrection, he opens for us the way to a new life. This new life is above all justification that reinstates us in God's grace, 'so that as Christ was raised from the dead by the glory of the Father, we too might walk in newness of life'" (*CCC*, 654). I know that in the midst of our struggles, we have so much to be grateful for. God has blessed each of us, but he's not done—he has more for us.

Pause & REFLECT

Take some time to reflect on the diagram below.

Where in your life are you experiencing suffering?

Where in your life are you or have you experienced a spiritual death?

Where in your life have you or do you desire to experience resurrection?

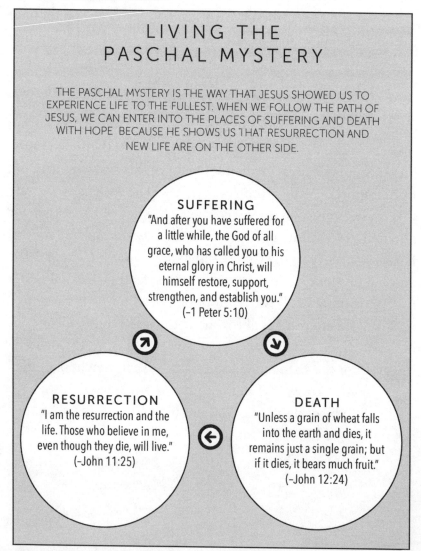

LIVING THE
PASCHAL MYSTERY

THE PASCHAL MYSTERY IS THE WAY THAT JESUS SHOWED US TO
EXPERIENCE LIFE TO THE FULLEST. WHEN WE FOLLOW THE PATH OF
JESUS, WE CAN ENTER INTO THE PLACES OF SUFFERING AND DEATH
WITH HOPE BECAUSE HE SHOWS US THAT RESURRECTION AND
NEW LIFE ARE ON THE OTHER SIDE.

SUFFERING
"And after you have suffered for
a little while, the God of all
grace, who has called you to his
eternal glory in Christ, will
himself restore, support,
strengthen, and establish you."
(–1 Peter 5:10)

RESURRECTION
"I am the resurrection and the
life. Those who believe in me,
even though they die, will live."
(–John 11:25)

DEATH
"Unless a grain of wheat falls
into the earth and dies, it
remains just a single grain; but
if it dies, it bears much fruit."
(–John 12:24)

Chapter 7

JESUS THE TRUTH

In September 2015, my son Judah, who had recently turned ten, suddenly fell ill and we had to take him to the hospital. After running some tests, the doctor quickly concluded that it was an appendicitis and they needed to get Judah into surgery as soon as possible. A couple of years prior to that, my daughter Maria had to get her appendix out, and it was a pretty smooth experience. Surgery and a couple of days at the hospital, and she was good to go, so I was expecting a similar situation with our son. Unfortunately, this time it was a vastly different experience, one that ended up being very traumatic for all of us.

His surgery appointment was delayed several times, and we ended up waiting from early in the morning until almost midnight for him to go into the operating room. He was in excruciating pain, and as a parent, it's the worst thing to watch your child suffer when there is nothing you can do to help them. I was at the hospital alone because my husband was at home taking care of our other two children. After he was finally taken into surgery, I paced back and forth in the waiting room with growing anxiety as the time surpassed when the doctor told me she would call. At 2:00 a.m., I finally got the phone call. Judah was out of surgery, but the doctor said it ended up being quite complicated because his appendix had actually ruptured and released toxic bacteria into his abdomen. She said the surgery went well, but there was a chance she wasn't able to get all the bacteria and it could cause major issues.

Later that morning, Judah was doing significantly worse than he was before the surgery. He was vomiting and fevered. He was reacting poorly to his medication, hallucinating, scared, and still in a lot of pain. For three days I watched Judah continue to decline, and seemingly no one was there to help. The nurses and doctor didn't seem to have any idea of what to do. I was trying my hardest to find what medication could help and find some solution, but honestly, I was scared because I hadn't seen any of my children get this sick and continue to get worse instead of better. I prayed and prayed, but I felt so alone.

The old lie that I believed about God being distant and unwilling to help me was still very active in my life at that point and was attacking my mind and doubt with increasing strength. On the fourth night, I was lying in a makeshift bed next to Judah praying and listening to worship music. A song called "Pieces" by Amanda Cook came on, and as I wrestled with doubt, fear, and lies, the truth contained in the words of her song began to break through the cycle of negative thoughts. The Holy Spirit began to bring peace and light into my darkness as she sang about the truth of who God is. That he is faithful, that he doesn't play games with our lives, and that he desires our greatest good.

As I allowed her words in the song to become my prayer, it opened my heart up to the goodness of God. The truth that this song was reminding us of is that God is Love and he is good and was not abandoning us. I felt Jesus inviting me to proclaim scripture out loud and sing these songs of worship in his room as a prayer over Judah. I didn't know where to even start, so I asked God to show me. What jumped into my mind was Psalm 41 which I had never read before. I closed the door to the room so no one would think I was crazy, opened my Bible, stretched out my hand over my son, and read the beginning of Psalm 41:1–3 aloud:

> Happy are those who consider the poor;
> the LORD delivers them in the day of trouble.
> The LORD protects them and keeps them alive;
> they are called happy in the land.
> You do not give them up to the will of their enemies.
> The LORD sustains them on their sickbed;
> in their illness you heal all their infirmities.

It was clear that although I didn't know what to pray, God was teaching me and giving me the words and the truth to proclaim.

For the next hour, I prayed through tears, proclaiming out loud scriptures of healing and God's promises. I sang songs of worship that invoked the Holy Spirit, that were filled with the truth of God's power, care, and provision. I could feel the atmosphere in the room shifting and hope begin to rise in my heart. It wasn't just a hope that Judah would get better, it was hope in the person of Jesus, hope in his power and promise. I was finally able to surrender my son to the One I could trust him with. No matter what was going to happen, I knew the Creator of the universe was with me, and he was capable of holding me through whatever was going to happen, even the worst. I had dispelled the lie that God is distant, uncaring.

The next morning Judah woke up, surprisingly filled with light. His fever was gone, his eyes looked bright, and within a couple of minutes, a huge smile appeared on his face. There was my boy! Something big had shifted, and by noon that day, the doctor said we were good to go home! I was utterly shocked at how quickly things turned around. God's healing had come through the night, and his joy had come in the morning (see Psalm 30:1–5).

As you're reading this, I'm very aware that you might be thinking, "Well this isn't how things have turned out for me." I get it, trust me; not everything in our lives ends with good outcomes. In light of that, I want to call this to mind from chapter 1: healing is always about intimacy—not just the removal of pain. This is no truer than with God himself. His deepest desire is to have you abide in him—to intimately bear your soul to him, entrusting him to care for every part of your life. I can't promise this will be pain free because there is a huge difference between asking God for what we desire versus expecting him to do what we want as if we are putting our order in at a drive-through. Deep relationship is the goal, not getting what we asked for.

Drawing close to and abiding in God in
the midst of the pain of life heals some
of our separation from him.

My son's physical healing isn't actually what I want you to pull out of this story; rather, I want to bring to your attention the healing I experienced from the lies and doubt that were assaulting my mind and heart. What God taught me about the power of declaring scripture and the truth out loud has been a weapon I have gained in my spiritual arsenal, and this weapon has wielded incredible power and authority in my life and those whom I pray for.

Human beings are fascinating. We are made of so many parts, a beautiful composition of body and soul. All unique, yet some things are true about every human person, namely, that our bodies and souls are one. When they separate, we call that death. The body reveals the soul and, as Pope John Paul II said, "The body, and it alone, is capable of making visible what is invisible, the spiritual and divine."[1] So, naturally what is inside comes out in a variety of ways in and through our bodies. What is in our hearts will seek to find its way out in and through the body and through our voice, facial expressions, emotional display, and body language.

As human beings, we often feel tortured when we cannot express what is in our hearts. Movies show us these moments so beautifully, as in the 2005 version of *Pride and Prejudice* when Mr. Darcy, agonized by his intense love for Elizabeth, climbs the misty hills and, as the sun breaks through, pained with vulnerability, professes his love for her.[2] And how many songs have been written about love and loss in an attempt to express what is in the heart of a lover? A couple getting married has to declare their love and vows for everyone to hear. There are some things we need to say out loud, not because God can't understand what is in our hearts but for ourselves and for others. *When we allow the truth to move from our hearts to our lips, it changes us, and what is more important than speaking the truth in relation to God?*

We see this overflow of the heart from the saints and within scripture in such beautiful ways. King David all throughout the Psalms is crying out to God with his voice, in both praise and supplication. In Psalm 28:6–7, he says, "Blessed be the Lord, for he has heard the sound of my pleadings. The Lord is my strength and my shield; in him my heart trusts; so I am helped, and my heart exults, and with my song I give thanks to him." And in Psalm 40:9–10 he says, "I have told the glad news of deliverance in the great congregation; see, I have not restrained my lips, as you know, O Lord. I have not hidden your saving help within my heart, I have spoken of your faithfulness and your salvation; I have not concealed your steadfast love and your faithfulness."

We hear the love, the lament, the longing within the heart of St. Augustine, who has turned from a sinner into a lover from a personal encounter with God. So great is his experience that his heart cannot contain it, and he is compelled to put words to it:

> Late have I loved you, O Beauty ever ancient, ever new, late have I loved you! You were within me, but I was outside, and it was there that I searched for you. In my unloveliness I plunged into the lovely things which you created. You were with me, but I was not with you. Created things kept me from you; yet if they had not been in you they would have not been at all. You called, you shouted, and you broke through my deafness. You flashed, you shone, and you dispelled my blindness. You breathed your fragrance on me; I drew in breath and now I pant for you. I have tasted you, now I hunger and thirst for more. You touched me, and I burned for your peace.[3]

And Our Lady has the most beautiful proclamation of the goodness of God in her Magnificat as she prays aloud, "My soul magnifies the Lord, and my spirit rejoices in God my Savior, for he has looked with favor on the lowliness of his servant. Surely, from now on all generations will call me blessed; for the Mighty One has done great things for me, and holy is his name" (Lk 1:47–49).

Words have power, and as scripture teaches us, "Death and life are in the power of the tongue" (Prv 28:21). We have all experienced moments when our hearts have been shattered and we have been deeply blessed by someone's words. When we apply the power of God's truth to the lies and the questions about ourselves and God that we have deep in our hearts, it can bring about breakthrough and healing. God's word has a power like no other words: "For the word of God is living and active, sharper than any two-edged sword, piercing to the division of soul and of spirit, of joints and of marrow, and discerning the thoughts and intentions of the heart" (Heb 4:12). There is a spiritual component that cannot be underestimated because in this life there is flesh and spirit. As spiritual beings, we can speak truth into the spiritual force of lies, death, hatred, anxiety, and bondage.

Speaking the truth into the lies is speaking God's very presence into them, for he alone is the truth.

One of the most powerful prayers we have as ammunition against the enemy is simply the name of Jesus. The *Catechism* so beautifully teaches us that "his name is the only one that contains the presence it signifies. Jesus is the Risen One, and whoever invokes the name of Jesus is welcoming the Son of God who loved him and who gave himself up for him" (*CCC*, 2666).

Over the last several years, especially in my greatest times of pain, this has become my favorite prayer. Just speaking the name of Jesus out loud has more power than any other words we can say.

His presence accompanies his name,
and his presence is what we so
desperately need.

When I'm interceding for someone, when I'm at a loss how to pray, and when I'm so weak and have nothing left, I speak the name of Jesus, over and over again. It becomes a rhythm, like a heartbeat prayer with each breath, Jesus. The Prince of Peace, Emmanuel, the Savior, the Light of the World, the Redeemer, who is truly present in all of his power, when we call upon his name.

A key to practically applying this is to begin to memorize key scriptures that speak to the themes where we need the truth of God to break the power of the lies. A few years ago, I bought a chalkboard for my kitchen where I could write a scripture of the month that the whole family would see each day and memorize. I've used scripture cards and written them on sticky notes on my bathroom mirror, but mostly I have spent time with my Bible, highlighting the texts that speak to me.

The fundamental principle is to find the
scriptures that specifically oppose the
lies that are unique to you.

For example, when I have struggled with the lie that God won't answer me and is far away, I consistently turn to Psalm 18:1–19: "In my distress I called upon the Lord to my God I cried for help. From his temple he heard my voice, and my cry to him reached his ears . . . the Lord was my support. He brought me out into a broad place; he delivered me, because he delighted in me." When I have struggled for a reason to have hope, I have clung to the words in Lamentations 3:21–23: "But I call this to mind as my reason for hope, the steadfast love of the Lord never ceases, his mercies never come to an end; they are new every morning; great is your faithfulness." When I needed to know God hasn't forgotten me, I have turned to Isaiah 49:14–16: "But Zion said, 'The Lord has forsaken me, my Lord has forgotten me.' Can a woman forget her nursing child, or show no compassion for the child of her womb? Even these may forget, yet I will not forget you. See, I have inscribed you on the palms of my hands."

Day after day we are bombarded with lies and deceit from the enemy. Those lies are particularly present when we experience hardships, relationship disruptions, people being cruel, rejection, and many other things that wound our hearts. The discipline and practice of taking time each day to immerse ourselves in the truth has never been more vital to us thriving. We have to be willing to pursue practical ways that we can proclaim the powerful truth of Christ be spoken into and over our lives, circumstances, pain, and lies.

Jesus is the Truth, and the more we lean into his truth, the less power the lies will have over us. We are invited to come out of the shadows and to live in the authority of our sonship and daughterhood in God. We are constantly surrounded by lies that are spoken in our hearts, our minds, our culture, the media, and our relationships, and often we are beaten down by it. It's time to take a stand. To ward off the attacks of the enemy, we must take a defensive posture and arm ourselves with God's truth, proclaim the truth out loud, and claim the victory of Christ over the enemy in our lives.

Pause & REFLECT

Take some time to journal and reflect on the following questions:

> What theme do you need to memorize a scripture about? Consider going on the internet and searching scriptures with that theme, such as hope, love, or mercy.

> Declaring the truth in scripture is a powerful weapon against the enemy's lies. Take some time each day praying with scripture and read it out loud. In what area of your life do you need the Truth to be spoken?

> Here are a few scripture suggestions to pray with and declare aloud:

Do not fear, for I have redeemed you;
 I have called you by name, *you are mine.*
When you pass through the waters, I will be with you;
 and through the rivers, they shall not overwhelm you;
when you walk through fire you shall not be burned,
 and the flame shall not consume you.
For I am the LORD your God,
 the Holy One of Israel, your Savior.
I give Egypt as your ransom,
 Ethiopia and Seba in exchange for you.
Because you are precious in my sight,
 and honored, and *I love you.* (Is 43:1–4, emphasis mine)

There is no fear in love, but perfect love casts out fear. (1 Jn 4:18)

The LORD, your God, is in your midst,
    a warrior who gives victory;
he will rejoice over you with gladness,
    he will renew you in his love. (Zep 3:17)

As far as the east is from the west,
    so far he removes our sins from us. (Ps 103:12)

For surely I know the plans I have for you, says the LORD, plans for your welfare and not for harm, to give you a future with hope. Then when you call upon me and come and pray to me, I will hear you. When you search for me, you will find me; if you seek me with all your heart. (Jer 29:11–13)

I have told you these things so that in me you may have peace. In this world you will have trouble, but take heart! I have overcome the world. (Jn 16:33)

The thief comes to steal and kill and destroy. I have come that you might have life and have it abundantly. (Jn 10:10)

But Zion said, "The LORD has forsaken me,
    my Lord has forgotten me."
Can a woman forget her nursing child,
    or show no compassion for the child of her womb?
Even these may forget,
    yet I will not forget you.
See, I have inscribed you on the palms of my hands. (Is 49:14–16)

But I call this to mind
    as my reason for hope,
the steadfast love of the LORD never ceases,
    his mercies never come to an end;

they are new every morning;
    great is your faithfulness. (Lam 3:21–23)

I am the vine, you are the branches. Those who abide in me
and I in them bear much fruit because apart from me you
can do nothing. (Jn 15:5)

Chapter 8

JESUS THE LIFE

A couple of years ago we bought nine acres of land with my parents. We went through the amazing process of designing and building a home where we could all live and make memories for a lifetime. Prior to purchasing the property, the previous owner decided to cut down all the mature trees, leaving the land bare. It made for an amazing view of the northern Cascade mountain range, but we knew that when we built the house, we would plant new trees soon after. When the first spring came around, we planted red maples, dogwoods, cherry blossoms, weeping willows, giant redwoods, cedars, a magnolia, hibiscus, and an oak that I hope will be a legacy tree for our great-grandkids one day. To help these trees thrive we had to set up watering systems, purchase watering bags, and make sure they had the right soil and the right amount of sunlight in order to survive the hot summer months ahead. There are certain things trees need to thrive, and without those essentials, they will wither and die.

Every human person also has essential needs in order to thrive at each stage of life. They differ slightly according to the

uniqueness of the masculine and feminine heart, but each need
is necessary and important for the individual to be nurtured in
a loving environment that leads to maturity and the experience
of healthy adulthood. When we think of what a person needs
to live, we initially think through the lens of what we believe
to be the most important: our physical needs such as food,
shelter, and water. Of course, these are vital to existence, but
just as important,

---

we have emotional and spiritual needs
to meet in order to have a healthy
development.

One is not more important than the other; they must all work
together to lay the foundation of a secure identity. This foundation can be built upon to achieve mature adulthood, where
the person is capable of making a sincere gift of themselves to
the world. "True freedom is measured by readiness to serve and
by the gift of self. It is so important to understand our human
nature, and that grace builds upon nature," Pope Benedict XVI
said. "Therefore, in order to educate in truth, it is necessary
first and foremost to know who the human person is, to know
human nature."[1]

One of the most foundational needs of the human person is
attachment. In my personal reading of it, the core of attachment
theory is that each human person needs to attach to parents
or a primary caregiver for healthy emotional, psychological,
and physical development. Without a secure attachment or if
the child attaches to an unstable or unhealthy adult, they will
experience difficulties in many aspects of their development
and overall stability. The relational foundation that each person

has is essential for the health and success of the rest of their life that is built upon it.

When we designed and constructed our house, we did a lot of research because we wanted to build something that would last and become our forever home. We didn't want to skimp on the important things, so we concluded it was worth the extra money to invest in the best foundation technology we could afford: insulated concrete forms. Essentially, they create an exceptionally strong foundation through a combination of concrete, steel reinforcements, and insulation that results in the house being incredibly energy efficient and able to withstand immense force. Everything else was built upon the strength of this foundation and is more secure as a result.

Imagine if we built our home with sections of the foundation missing. At the very least it would have significant weakness in those areas and begin to crumble when enough pressure was applied through weight or natural disasters. The greatest risk would be that the house would completely collapse. A strong foundation is formed within the human person, withstanding the force and storms of life, when our physical, emotional, and spiritual needs are repeatedly met by healthy people we have attached to. The fruit of these experiences goes deep into our hearts and secures us in ourselves and in the world.

Love secures us.

As we reflect on our developmental and emotional history, it is necessary to acknowledge that it will undoubtedly uncover some areas where we have deficiencies, places in our hearts where needs weren't met at that time. This does not always mean our parents are to blame or that it should damage relationships.

They were quite possibly doing the best they could with what they had to offer. It also does not mean we are being ungrateful for our childhood and all we were given. As a parent, I know I love my kids with all my heart, but I do miss things that they need sometimes, I hurt them unintentionally, and I sometimes communicate messages to them that I don't intend. No human parent is perfect, but the impact of what parents miss cannot be overlooked. Healing is needed in those places. For some of us though, we experienced deep trauma from the people who were supposed to love us the most. This has inevitably affected our relationships with them, and sometimes we need to distance ourselves to stay safe. In the most horrible situations as well as in the seemingly small, God can bring healing and does not abandon us.

> But now thus says the LORD,
>   he who created you, O Jacob,
>   he who formed you, O Israel:
> Do not fear, for I have redeemed you;
>   I have called you by name, you are mine.
> When you pass through the waters, I will be with you;
>   and through the rivers, they shall not overwhelm you;
> when you walk through fire you shall not be burned,
>   and the flame shall not consume you.
> For I am the LORD your God,
>   the Holy One of Israel, your Savior.
> I give Egypt as your ransom,
>   Ethiopia and Seba in exchange for you.
> Because you are precious in my sight,
>   and honored, and I love you. (Is 43:1–4)

Acknowledging that we have areas of deficiency within us has a threefold purpose. First, it fosters humility and grounds us in our vital dependence on God. Second, it gives insight into the possible roots of our current sin, brokenness, unrest, or unhealthy styles of relating. Third, it opens up the door for Christ to come in and restore what was needed at those stages.

Restoration happens when we allow ourselves to enter into a secure attachment with God our Father who can heal all the deficiencies we have experienced along the way.

Recall the words of the *Catechism of the Catholic Church*: "No one is Father as God is Father" (239). God's love is perfect and can heal any wound. The *Catechism* also says, "God's love for Israel (his chosen people) is compared to a father's love for his son. His love for his people is stronger than a mothers' for her children. God loves his people more than a bridegroom his beloved; his love will be victorious over even the worst infidelities and will extend to his most precious gift; 'God so loved the world that he gave his only Son' (Jn 3:16)" (*CCC*, 219). No matter what our story holds, we were made to be one with God, to be *securely attached to him*. Living out of that secure attachment with God is what it means to abide in him. The fruit of that attachment to God is that what was lost through our parents and caregivers can be restored by him.

Contemplate the following charts that lay out the essential pieces of the development of the feminine and masculine hearts. These apply to men and women irrespective of their vocation, for all are called to either the spiritual or the physical vocation of bride/groom and mother/father. Each of them is slightly nuanced, but the stages build upon each other in the same manner. As you take time to reflect on each stage of your development, notice what the experiential need of that stage is and ponder whether that need was met in your life.

DEVELOPMENT OF THE MASCULINE HEART

STAGE	EXPERIENTIAL NEED	RESULT (EMOTIONAL MATURITY)
FATHER	I'M FULLY ALIVE WHEN I GIVE LIFE TO OTHERS	GENEROUS LIFE GIVER
HUSBAND	I'M FULLY ALIVE WHEN I OFFER MY MASCULINITY TO MY BRIDE	SELFLESS LOVER
MAN	I KNOW WHAT I'M ALL ABOUT AND I HAVE A MISSION	PURPOSEFUL STRENGTH
YOUNG MAN	I HAVE WHAT IT TAKES AND I KNOW THAT I'M CAPABLE	CONFIDENT AND CAPABLE (SELF-MASTERY)
BOY	I AM THE BELOVED SON; I AM SEEN AND KNOWN	SECURITY AND TRUST
MALE HUMAN PERSON	I'M OK AND IT'S GOING TO BE OK	SAFETY

DEVELOPMENT OF THE FEMININE HEART

STAGE	EXPERIENTIAL NEED	RESULT (EMOTIONAL MATURITY)
MOTHER	I'M FULLY ALIVE WHEN I RECEIVE AND GIVE BIRTH TO NEW LIFE	GENEROUS LIFE GIVER
WIFE	I'M FULLY ALIVE WHEN I OFFER MY FEMINITY TO MY BRIDEGROOM	VULNERABLE AND RECEPTIVE LOVER
WOMAN	I KNOW WHAT I'M ALL ABOUT AND I HAVE A MISSION	SENSITIVITY AND STRENGTH
YOUNG WOMAN	I AM A GIFT; I AM ENOUGH	TREASURED
GIRL	I AM SEEN AND I AM DELIGHTFUL	SECURITY AND TRUST
FEMALE HUMAN PERSON	I'M OK AND IT'S GOING TO BE OK	SAFETY

It's important to understand that just as our stages of physical development build upon one another, so does our emotional development. It reminds me of the wooden block game Jenga, which challenges players to remove the blocks from the tower and placing them at the top of the structure—all without bringing the tower down. Before long you will notice that when wooden blocks are missing and there are spaces in the tower, it becomes unstable and soon impossible for you to continue building the tower. Similarly for us, if there are deficiencies, where our experiential and emotional needs were not met, we are unable to continue developing fully in those areas and we can experience instability and an inability to continue growing in maturity. This usually happens over time and we may not understand in our current stage of life why we struggle in a particular way. For example, we may have an insatiable longing for validation or suffer anxiety because we never feel secure. When we see what has been missed, it can explain why we do what we do and the aches within our hearts.

Wherever we have needs in our past that weren't met, we will likely experience a lack of emotional maturity in those areas of our current stage of life.

There have been times that we hear someone say to a grown adult, "Why are you acting like a child?" Often there is truth within those words. There are likely parts within each of us that haven't emotionally matured past eight or fifteen or twenty years old. The hopeful truth to know is that God can fill in these gaps. For example, I have a friend who grew up with a very distant and harsh father. He was never affirmed by his dad or told that he was loved; no matter how many successes he achieved in his life, his dad never told him that he was proud of him. The lack of a loving father resulted in a huge wound within this young man. Because he didn't have the secure love of his father, nor did he have the affirmation along the way to believe that he had what it took to navigate life successfully, he was very insecure and found himself aching for and grasping after affirmation and acceptance in many other relationships in his life. He didn't know why he struggled so much to be confident and secure. It was only when he had some deep experiences of God the Father speaking into his identity as beloved son and meeting other men, who became spiritual fathers for him, that he had was able to experience restoration. The fruit of that restoration led to maturity and an ability for him to more fully engage in the roles of husband and father in his own life.

When we come to God with the areas within us that need to be seen, known, and loved, we open the door for him to meet our deepest needs. He can also send other people into our lives to fill the gaps where we need love, acceptance, and security. Even as adults, our unmet needs from our childhood can be healed and made whole, by God and a loving community or spiritual family. Maturity is a fruit of healing, purity, and secure love.

At the foundation of our human development, we have a need to know and experience that we are okay and that everything is going to be okay. When this need is met, the result is safety. This safety comes when infants bond and attach to a parent or primary caregiver through frequent, close loving contact and repeated experiences of comfort, love, reassurance, and being protected and cared for. As I discussed previously in chapter 5, our relationship with our parents sets the tone for all future relationships, including God.

This need for safety begins in the womb. We all know that a mother who uses drugs and has poor nutrition will affect a baby in her womb, but what we may not know is that a mother's emotional health negatively or positively affects the baby within her womb as well. For example, if a mother was struggling with depression and feelings of not wanting her baby while she was pregnant, those intense emotions affect the baby in the womb. A deep-rooted belief about being unwanted can get planted within the heart of the infant, which often results in that child becoming an adult who struggles with feelings of abandonment or being unwanted in various relationships, even if those relationships are full of love. This concept carries through all the stages of our development; the impact of our emotional environment from the moment of our conception and throughout our childhood and development significantly affects our experience and level of emotional maturity as an adult.

As mentioned in chapter 3, we all have a story, and we all have areas where there are deficiencies. When we see what is lacking, we have an opportunity to draw closer to God and allow him to fill the voids with his love, truth, and life. We obviously can't change the past, but we can invite Jesus, God the Father, and the Holy Spirit into the areas of our lives where we did not experience healthy attachment or stability and experience healing by attaching to and abiding in God, who is the healthy, stable, perfect Father. Our hearts were made to attach to him, and he is the only one who can provide the perfection of all that we need now and have always needed from the beginning.

Although challenging and uncomfortable, it is vital that we acknowledge difficult parts of our history. We must allow ourselves to grow in self-knowledge while being on guard against self-absorption. There are many people I know who have been going to counseling for quite some time. For some, as they grow in the understanding of the wounded parts of their story and invite Jesus in to heal and restore, they are experiencing change and lasting fruit. There are others, however, who have gotten lost in a cycle of focusing so much on their wounds that they have lost hope and lost sight of the path forward. Instead of holding the truth of Jesus who is offering healing, comfort, and restoration, they are stuck in a place where they can only see and experience their pain. As I see it, they are allowing their identity to be determined by their pain and by labels, instead of by the Father who desperately loves them as his beloved children. In the journey of healing, it's essential to keep our eyes fixed on Jesus, our hope.

Self-knowledge promotes humility, faith, and dependence on God, while self-absorption promotes hopelessness, self-reliance, and a "woe is me" mentality. Self-absorption leads to turning our eyes from God to seek answers in idols, others, and self. Instead of turning inward, we are invited to turn our face toward the gaze of God.

Just as an infant bonds with their parents through close eye-to-eye contact, so too must we allow ourselves to see and be seen by the gaze of God. God wants us to truly know him, not as *the* Father but as *our* father. He is not the result of our impressions and doubts, nor is he the reason all has gone wrong in our lives. He is the author of life, not the author of death. He's a good and faithful father who desires closeness, connection, and attachment. "I drew them with human cords, with bands of l love; I fostered them like one who raises an infant to his cheek; yet, though I stopped to feed my child, they did not know that I was their healer" (Hos 11:4).

Abiding in the presence of God and in the gaze of the source of our life is not compatible with a life of sin. It doesn't mean we don't sin, but a life filled with mortal sin that severs our relationship with the Trinity is incompatible with intimacy and abiding in God. When we are in an abiding relationship with God who is love, it causes a movement outward, wherein the art of loving the other has primary importance and the love of self becomes last. As shown in the charts above, this is the result of maturity. When we are safe and secure in our identity, when we know who we are, and when we know we are seen and loved for who we are, we are able to give freely of ourselves to the world and open wide the door to be transformed into the image of Christ. As scripture says, "And all of us, with unveiled faces, seeing the glory of the Lord as though reflected in a mirror, are being transformed into the same image from one degree of glory to another; for this comes from the Lord, the Spirit" (2 Cor 3:18).

As we are being transformed into the image of Christ, we experience being fully alive because this is who we were meant to be. This is when our lives become fragrant with the fruits of the Spirit instead of the darkness of sin. It is true that you will know the health of a tree by its fruit, and you will also know the level of transformation within the human heart by the visibility of the fruits of the Spirit.

> Now the works of the flesh are obvious: fornication, impurity, licentiousness, idolatry, sorcery, enmities, strife, jealousy, anger, quarrels, dissensions, factions, envy, drunkenness, carousing, and things like these. I am warning you, as I warned you before: those who do such things will not inherit the kingdom of God. By contrast, the fruit of the Spirit is love, joy, peace, patience, kindness, generosity, faithfulness, gentleness, and self-control. There is no law against such things. And those who belong to Christ Jesus have crucified the flesh with its passions and desires. If we live by the Spirit, let us also be guided by the Spirit. (Gal 5:19–25)

Joy and stability come with real maturity. The emotionally mature person has their identity rooted in being a beloved son/daughter of the Father, and they are able to live from the hope that "all will be well." This is when we know deep in our bones that we belong to a father who loves us, who is providing for us, and who will carry us through any difficulty we encounter. It moves us from our faith being shaken when suffering occurs to a disposition of surrender, which we see within Jesus in relationship with the Father. In the most intense time of suffering, Jesus said, "My Father, if it be possible, let this cup pass from me; nevertheless, not as I will, but as you will" (Mt 26:39, ESV). I love that word "nevertheless"; it speaks to the radical abandonment of his will to the will of the Father. He is saying, this is what I want, but if it's not what you want, Father, I surrender to you and I trust you. I want your will more than my own. As we find ourselves secure in the Father, we can let go of our way and live a life of unconditional trust.

Jesus speaks so clearly about attachment in the Gospel of John.

> I am the true vine, and my Father is the vine grower. . . . Abide in me as I abide in you. Just as the branch cannot bear fruit by itself unless it abides in the vine, neither can you unless you abide in me. I am the vine, you are the branches. Those who abide in me and I in them bear much fruit, because apart from me you can do nothing. Whoever does not abide in me is thrown away like a branch and withers; such branches are gathered, thrown into the fire, and burned. If you abide in me, and my words abide in you, ask for whatever you wish, and it will be done for you. My Father is glorified by this, that you bear much fruit and become my disciples. As the Father has loved me, so I have loved you; abide in my love. If you keep my commandments, you will abide in my love, just as I

have kept my Father's commandments and abide in his love.
I have said these things to you so that my joy may be in you,
and that your joy may be complete. (Jn 15:1–11)

We are supposed to be like a branch attached to the vine.
When Jesus is our source of life and we are attached to him, we
will thrive and our joy will be complete.

The sacraments are practical ways that we can attach to God
as they make visible the invisible and communicate God's life
and grace to us. The Second Vatican Council teaches us that the
Eucharist is the pinnacle of the sacraments and is "the source
and summit of the Christian life"[2] (*Lumen Gentium*, 11). In our
pursuit of a "life to the full" (Jn 10:10), receiving the body and
blood of Jesus is essential because we are then filled with his
very life. We can't get any closer to God than to have his body in
our bodies, becoming truly one flesh with him. In his pastoral
visit to Poland, Pope John Paul II said,

> Christ came into the world to bestow upon man divine life.
> He not only proclaimed the Good News but he also insti-
> tuted the Eucharist which is to make present until the end of
> time his redeeming mystery. And as the means of expressing
> this he chose the elements of nature—the bread and wine,
> the food and drink that man must consume to maintain his
> life. The Eucharist is precisely this food and drink. This food
> contains in itself all the power of the Redemption wrought by
> Christ. In order to live, man needs food and drink. In order
> to gain eternal life man needs the Eucharist. This is the food
> and drink that transforms man's life and opens before him
> the way to eternal life. By consuming the Body and Blood of
> Christ, man bears within himself, already on this earth, the
> seed of eternal life, for the Eucharist is the sacrament of life
> in God. Christ says: "As the living Father sent me, and I live

because of the Father, so he who eats me will live because of me." (Jn 6:57)[2]

Jesus is the way, the truth, and the life. He has opened every door for us to experience the fullness of life that he is offering. As we experience a deeper connection with him, grow closer to him, and abide in him, we become fully human and fully alive.

Jesus wants to come into all the places in our lives where we have deficiencies and didn't get what we needed to thrive. Not only can he bring comfort and peace to those places within our hearts, but also he can heal and transform them so we can live in freedom as sons and daughters of a faithful father.

Pause & REFLECT

Take some time to pray through the chart that applies to you on p. 98 or p. 99. Invite the Holy Spirit to illuminate the things in your life that you needed at a certain stage and didn't receive. Invite Jesus to come into that void and to speak his Truth. Invite the Father to come into those little places of your heart and fill you with his love and fatherly blessing. (This is meant to be not a onetime exercise, but one you do regularly.)

Do we know that there is still a part of us that is a child, needing to be fathered by God?

It is exhausting when we try to keep it all together, to look so strong and capable. Take some time to reflect and journal about this dynamic in your life.

What words of delight and love do you desire to hear from God the Father?

Chapter 9

ESSENTIALS IN THE JOURNEY OF HEALING

As a child, my favorite books were the Chronicles of Narnia series by C. S. Lewis. I wasn't usually a huge reader, but I vividly remember laying in my bed at age ten, unable to put down the Narnia series because it was so riveting. I loved that the animals could talk, that there was a mysterious and magical world, the epic battle between good and evil, and the adventure. It wasn't until I revisited these stories later in life that I was opened up to the rich Christian imagery and themes hidden within their pages. One of my favorite stories that relate to healing and restoration is in the book *The Voyage of the Dawn Treader*.

The story begins with the siblings, Lucy and Edmund, visiting their cousin, Eustace, at his home for the summer. One day the three children were pulled through a magical portal into an ocean in the world of Narnia, but this time their cousin was with them. They were soon rescued by a ship filled with people

Lucy and Edmund immediately recognized as their friends. Their cousin, Eustace, was a very bratty child. He was self-centered, disagreeable, and a bully. No matter how nice everyone was to him, he disliked them all and always found something to complain about. We don't know what led up to Eustace becoming such a difficult person, but I imagine he had a story too.

When they finally found land, everyone pitched in to help repair the damage that the stormy seas had inflicted on the ship—everyone but Eustace. Instead of working, Eustace decided that he deserved a break. He took a walk and found an old dragon den that was filled with treasure. Greed and pride overwhelmed his heart. He grabbed a gold bracelet, put it on his arm, and fell asleep. When he awoke, he was shocked to find that he himself had turned into a dragon and the gold bracelet was now digging painfully into his arm. Scared and embarrassed, he returned to the beach to get help from his cousins and the ship's crew. No matter what they tried, nothing could change Eustace back into a boy. As a dragon, Eustace became profoundly aware of how ugly he was, how disgusting he had become, and humbled by how kind everyone continued to be to him despite his disfigurement. Eustace had nowhere to turn and was filled with shame and fear, until the arrival of the one who would change everything. Aslan, a massive and beautiful lion, had come to set him free.

Aslan, the Christ figure in the series, approached Eustace and invited him to follow him into the woods, where he led him to a pool of water. Aslan asked Eustace to enter into the water and wash off the scales. As Eustace scratched and clawed at his thick dragon skin, one layer and then a second peeled off, but it was not enough. Aslan looked at Eustace and told him that he would have to lay down and allow his lion claw to "undress" him and remove the dragon skin. He lifted up his claws and tore through the many layers of dragon skin. Eustace cried in pain, but after a moment all the layers fell to the ground and all that was left was Eustace, the boy. Eustace bathed in the healing water, and all of his pain went away. Aslan gave him new clothes and walked him back to his friends. As Eustace returned, he was changed and everyone could immediately see it. He was humble and kind, quieter, and softer in every way.[1]

This story is rich in symbolism, but it also provides a bit of a road map about essentials in the healing journey that I would like to elaborate on. The first is the importance of community. Just as Eustace isolated from everyone and wandered away, it is common for us, when we are in an unhealthy place, to distance ourselves from those who care about us, even God. We find comfort in solitude and being alone with our wounded parts and in hiding our vulnerability.

Several things can happen in the places where we isolate ourselves. Isolation is fertile ground for the enemy to plant lies, and when we make agreements with those lies, they turn into false beliefs that become deeply rooted within our hearts and minds. When we are alone, it is very difficult to distinguish the lies from the truth, and the loss of perspective can cause us to give in to victimhood and despair. It's only after Eustace comes back to the community that he is able to encounter Aslan and enter into healing. We desperately need a community and individuals within that community who can personally accompany us in our journey of healing. We need friends we can be brutally honest with, people who can speak words of hope and truth to us, counselors who can guide our hearts and minds, a spiritual director who is an expert of the soul, and other support people.

We also need connection with our regular Church community for worship and most importantly the sacraments.

We are not meant to journey in the Paschal Mystery alone.

Even Jesus had Simon of Cyrene to help him carry his Cross, his mother and the women of Jerusalem to comfort him, John the beloved standing with him till the end, and Mary Magdalene to be the first witness of the Resurrection.

The second essential we can learn from the story of Eustace is that there are moments when things on the inside get exposed, and we are invited to choose vulnerability. It's interesting that although the story depicts Eustace as suddenly becoming a dragon,

I believe he always had the "dragon" within.

In my interpretation, what was already on the interior of Eustace suddenly came out to the exterior, and all of his ugliness that was inside his heart took the form of a dragon.

I often wonder what I would look like if all of my ugliness or wounds on the inside appeared on my exterior. It's as though a layer was removed so Eustace could see his own disfigurement that he had been dealing with interiorly for some time. He was finally able to see his own need for a savior. This has to be a part of the healing process for each of us. We must allow what is on the inside to become visible; we need to let ourselves see it and let God see it. It is a coming into a deep acceptance of the reality of our story and inner world, our brokenness, our sin, our addiction, and the places where we have been victimized and are in pain. As we grow in compassion for ourselves, we realize our poverty and need for God, instead of self-hatred and shame that leads us into isolation.

This never feels good, but it is good. It's sort of like when a child skins their knee really badly and they cover it with their hands and don't want anyone to see or touch it—they don't even want to see it themselves—but unless the wound is seen and attended to, it will never heal properly. Being vulnerable about our distorted and imperfect parts, which we can't change on our own, leads to an openness to one who can, Jesus our Savior.

Don't be afraid to let the light of Christ into the darkness and the hidden places. He's not afraid of it. It is there that he wants to be and there that we need him the most.

The third essential in the healing journey is that we have to let go of self-reliance. We see this in the story when Eustace accepted the fact that he could not heal himself. He needed the community to prepare him and for Aslan to do the healing for him. This is so hard for us to come to grips with, especially those of us who pride ourselves on being strong, capable people who can "handle it." We were not meant to do it all, and truthfully, we can't do it all. Jesus says, "Abide in me as I abide in you. Just as the branch cannot bear fruit by itself unless it abides in the vine, neither can you unless you abide in me. I am the vine, you are the branches. Those who abide in me and

I in them bear much fruit, because apart from me you can do nothing" (Jn 15:4–5).

We are so good at fighting to do things ourselves and rejecting help. I remember when my daughter Eva was just two years old and we took her swimming. We would try to put on her life jacket before taking her to the pool, and she would scream and cry because she didn't want to put it on. Eventually, we gave up and I told her that instead of having to wear her life jacket, I would hold her in the pool. She started to cry again and yelled, "No, I do it!" She thought she could swim on her own like an Olympic champion, but I knew that if I didn't help her, she would immediately drown.

We can so often act like this when God or others try to help us. We are so convinced that doing it our way and doing it ourselves is best, but Jesus is the only one who has defeated death and risen from the grave, and he is the only one who can resurrect the dead and the broken places in us. There are also people God has commissioned to assist us in becoming open to the grace of God and working through the many blocks we have so that as we approach Jesus, we are receptive to his movements. We need good counselors, holy priests, spiritual directors, and friends of Jesus to accompany us to the healing. We see a great example of this in the Gospel of Luke 5:17–20 when a group of men made a hole in the roof of the house where Jesus was so they could lower their friend in and place him at the feet of Jesus to be healed.

This is the role of those who accompany us: to help us remove the blocks so we can come to the feet of Jesus and be healed.

The fourth essential that C. S. Lewis's story provides is the importance of identifying the false self and the true self within all of us. When Aslan has to "undress" Eustace, he removes the layers of dragon skin to reveal the real boy inside. Eustace isn't really a dragon, nor is his true identity in being as pernicious as he was to his friends. The dragon skin was a covering, a false identity, that was representative of his sin and wretchedness. The real Eustace was hiding inside, the sweet and kind boy Aslan uncovers. This is so rich for us to reflect on.

Like Adam and Eve in the garden who covered themselves with fig leaves, we have a covering over who we really are. That covering is closely attached to shame, and the Lord wants to remove it from us. He wants the true identity and glory of each of us to be revealed. We are not our sin or our failures; we are beloved children of the Creator of the universe.

We have glory and the song of heaven stamped in our bodies and breathed into our souls.

It is through our wounds and our sin that a false self has emerged to cover our real selves. The false self is made up of pain, shame, sin, our deficiencies, our wounds, our insecurities, our failures, our overcompensating, and our flaws.

The journey of healing involves uncovering the false self so the true self can emerge. You are glorious, chosen, royal, unrepeatable, and made by the hands of Love himself, with the

fingerprints of the Father upon you.
There is never a better time for us to
shed the false self than right now.

Freedom and living the full life are impossible if the real self is in bondage and hiding.

The last essential in the journey that we can draw from the story is accessing the sacramental life of the Church, which is represented when Eustace is cleansed by the water and dressed in new clothes. The *Catechism* teaches us that "the sacraments are perceptible signs (words and actions) accessible to our human nature. By the action of Christ and the power of the Holy Spirit, they make present efficaciously the grace that they signify" (*CCC*, 1084). God uses tangible signs, such as water at Baptism and bread in the Eucharist, to bestow his grace and presence to us. The sacraments are accessible to all of us and are avenues of nourishment, grace, healing, power, strength, and life, and they communicate the mystery of God's love and our union with him.

The sacraments aren't obligations or ceremonies; rather, they are encounters with Christ who is present in each one.

We cannot live the full life Christ is
offering us without the sacraments and
the grace contained within them.

They provide the very lifeblood of our spiritual life, where we abide with Christ and he with us. To say they are necessary for healing is a vast understatement. Some of us feel unworthy to receive the sacraments, and you know what? You're right.

None of us are worthy of anything that God offers to us, yet he has adopted us into his family. He is generous and desires to lavish his goodness upon us because he loves us. "You are a chosen race, a royal priesthood, a holy nation, a people for his own possession, that you may proclaim the excellencies of him who called you out of darkness into his marvelous light" (1 Pt 2:9). The sacraments are a pure, undeserved gift, available and meant for you and for me. Let us open wide the doors to Jesus who is waiting to encounter us in the sacraments.

These essentials in the journey of healing—community, allowing ourselves to be exposed, dependence on Jesus instead of self-reliance, identifying the false self and the true self, and partaking of the sacramental life of the Church—will help us if we actually incorporate them into our lives. As with all the practical applications I have mentioned in this book, they are tools to use, not good ideas to toss in a folder and forget about. We love a good quote and a good idea, but as Christians, we are encouraged to allow good seeds to be planted in good soil so they can take root and bear good fruit. So it is with the practical tools and essentials for the journey. The invitation is to move from thinking about them to actively pursuing them and using them. Scrolling social media isn't going to help us heal, but sitting in prayer, receiving the sacraments, growing in self-knowledge, and all the others will help us in the process of restoration.

Pause & REFLECT

Take some time to journal and reflect on the following questions:

What holds me back from making progress in the journey of restoration and healing?

What is one practical step I can take to pursue healing right now?

How would I describe my false self? How would I describe my true self?

Who is one trustworthy and equipped person I can reach out to for help in my healing journey this week?

Chapter 10

SIGNS OF GLORY

I was sixteen years old when I heard the news that my dad had been diagnosed with cancer, large-cell non-Hodgkin's lymphoma. A lump under his arm, which had been originally misdiagnosed, had dramatically grown, and when the new results came in, the doctors said he was already in stage 4. Stage 4 meant it had spread to other regions of his body and that he was in the most serious stage of the disease. He immediately started treatment, and I watched Dad go from a capable, full of life, successful CEO to a withering, frail, and very sick man.

Our lives changed instantly as everything fell into the periphery, and all we could focus on was Dad. We didn't have a cancer treatment center in our city, so my mom had to drive forty-five minutes to take him to the cancer clinic in Vancouver. He would have to stay there for a few days at a time for treatments and then come home and try to manage all of the horrible side effects. I was in shock, and I was scared. I felt paralyzed and didn't know how to react because I was suddenly faced with the realization that I didn't really even know my dad and I might lose him before getting the opportunity. He worked so hard for our family, such long hours, so much traveling, that I hadn't realized the distance that had grown between us. At that point, I knew him as my dad, but I didn't yet know him as my friend, as a person with a unique story of his own to share. I was so afraid I would lose him before I had the chance to know him.

We started praying like crazy, offering Masses and praying the Rosary, asking everyone we knew to intercede for him. As they ran tests to assess the gravity of his illness, we would pray at every step that cancer wouldn't be present in that area of his body, but it seemed our prayers were met with silence from God. Over a few weeks, we heard the cancer was in his lymph nodes, in his blood, his spleen, his bone marrow . . . it was everywhere. My heart was flooded with fear, discouragement, and hopelessness. Why was I even praying when God seemingly wasn't listening? Why did my prayers not have the outcome I wanted? The old wound was resurfacing as I heard the familiar lie that God was distantly watching but wasn't going to intervene. He could, but he wouldn't. In that lie were several layers of pain, feelings of abandonment, that God didn't care or love me, that he was okay with watching me suffer, and that my desires didn't matter to him. I felt completely powerless as I stood and watched my dad's health disintegrate before my eyes.

In the middle of this mess, I had the opportunity to go to World Youth Day in Denver and see Pope John Paul II. I was excited to go on the trip, but also, it was a chance to escape the pain of the situation with my dad. On that trip, I witnessed and personally experienced God moving powerfully, and something changed in my heart. Over the course of that week, a deep sense of peace surrounded me and began to settle my anxieties.

With the blessing of the peace of God and an awareness of his presence with me, I was able to come to a place of acceptance as I heard the Lord whisper in my heart, "Heather, no matter what happens, you are going to be okay. I am with you, and I'm never going to leave you." I was able to pray in response with sincerity, "Jesus, this is so painful, but I choose to trust you." I came back home with that deep peace that surpassed human understanding in my heart. I had faith that whether Dad lived or died, God would carry me through and I would be okay.

One night my dad was in the cancer clinic because they had asked him to come in for a scan to see a new clump of tumors they had found in his abdomen. The doctors had recently told him that his chances of survival were about 3 percent and that it was time for him to get his things in order because he wasn't going to live much longer. As he lay in his bed that night, waiting for his scan the next morning, he picked up a little New Testament that was on his nightstand. Up until that point my dad hadn't read the Bible much; he was a faithful Sunday Catholic, but his faith hadn't been very personal. He opened the Bible to a passage about the forgiveness and mercy of God. It touched his heart and for the first time gave him a deep sense of the love of God. He wanted to read more, so he opened the Bible to the book of Mark. It was the story of the healing of the leper, and it really spoke to my dad as he lay there, his own body riddled with disease. He placed the Bible on his chest, closed his eyes, and prayed, "Dear Lord Jesus, if you will it, please remove this spirit of cancer from me and replace it with your spirit of good health, wellness, and full recovery."

At that moment, something amazing happened. He described an experience of feeling like liquid energy was pouring into his eyes that flooded his entire body. He felt as if his body was shaking with the intensity of the experience. In fact, it was so intense that he had to open his eyes, and when he did everything stopped. It was so real and so powerful; he was left dumbfounded. What had just happened? An indescribable feeling of joy welled up within, and laughter erupted from him. Either God moved in a miraculous way, or he was losing his marbles.

The next morning, he went in for the tests and scans. When they finally finished, the doctor came in and said to my dad, "Well, Mr. McGuire, that was the most boring three hours of my life because there was nothing there." The previous tests had shown cancerous tumors throughout his body, but the latest scan showed that all of the cancer was completely gone. He was healed! A huge smile broke across my dad's face as he jumped out of bed and said, "Great! Can I go home now?" He came home that day, and from that moment on, all that we witnessed was the recovery and restoration of his health and body. Everything was coming back, his hair, his energy, his smiles, and his strength, but most importantly, my dad was back; he was home, and Jesus had miraculously healed him.

The joy of having Dad healed was tremendous, but the opportunity to have our relationship grow and deepen has been another incredible gift. Not only do I know him as my dad, but also we have grown a close friendship in the years since his healing. He is a loving grandfather to six grandchildren and just celebrated his fifty-fifth wedding anniversary with Mom. He has felt so much gratitude for what God has done, so just like the leper that was healed in the Bible, he has tried his best to say thank you to God. One of the primary ways he has done that was to start a foundation that supports more than fifty charities throughout the world. Instead of using what he had for selfish gain, his heart was inspired to show his gratitude to God by saving lives and helping those in need.

When God heals us, God also multiplies the fruit of that healing in the lives of those around us.

Ask for Miracles

In Dad's story, he didn't really think about asking for Jesus to heal him. In fact, he later told me that although he had prayed many times for other people, he had never asked for anything for himself. Despite the severe challenges in his life, he had always believed God had blessed him in so many ways so he felt unworthy to ask for anything else. He also didn't feel worthy because he hadn't had an encounter with the love of God in a personal way. It was only when he had opened up the scriptures that God poured his love into my dad's heart so deeply that it brought tears to his eyes. The experience of love and mercy led to an openness to ask God for healing. When we encounter the love of God, it gives us hope that he cares for us and has good things in store.

It's important to ask God for a miracle, and even if the answer isn't what we want, God is still good. I don't know why God healed my dad. There certainly have been thousands of times I've prayed for something and didn't get what I wanted, as I'm sure you have as well. In those times, when the answer isn't what I want, I've had to ask myself, does that mean God changed from good to not good? Is his goodness dependent on my approval or disapproval of how he answers my prayers? It's important to ask God for a miracle even if the answer isn't

We are invited to trust him, that even if things
we think they should, "all things work together
se who love God, who are called according to
purpose (Rom 8:28). Most importantly, depending on and
asking the Father for what we need fosters intimacy, which is
the real goal of healing.

I have seen, over and over again, that in the midst of all of
my storms, struggles, and pain, Jesus was there.

My situation doesn't always change,
but when I open my heart to him,
his presence, and his voice, my
perspective changes.

Why God chooses to heal some and not others is a question we
will all like to ask when we see him face-to-face, but I do know
this: the total removal of our pain, suffering, and tears is called
heaven. If God were to remove all of that for each person, we
would all be in heaven where "he will wipe away every tear from
their eyes, and death shall be no more, neither shall there be
mourning nor crying nor pain anymore" (Rv 21:4). We are not
there yet, so we wait, and in our waiting, he gives us miracles
as signs of hope.

Wounds to Scars

When Jesus rose from the dead, he began appearing to the disciples, but there was one, Thomas, who hadn't seen him yet. He
didn't believe the stories were true, he said: "Unless I see the
mark of the nails in his hands, and put my finger in the mark
of the nails and my hand in his side, I will not believe" (Jn
20:25). Jesus in his beautiful mercy and understanding comes

to Thomas to show him the scars on his hands and his side. Those scars, only a few days earlier, were wounds. Crucifixion wounds were a sign of shame and horror, but these wounds had healed; they were now scars and had become a sign of glory that pointed to the truth of the Resurrection. They were the sign that everything Jesus said and did was true, that he truly is the Son of God.

> Just as Jesus's wounds have become a sign of glory, he wants ours to become the same. Our wounds, which have been a sign of our shame or sin, once transformed by the healing power of God, are meant to be a sign to the world of the Good News of Christ.

In our culture, people love to share their story and speak their truth, especially on public platforms and social media. I've noticed that many of these stories are stories of victimhood or woundedness filled with indiscretion, a display of false vulnerability, and they often have no real redemption in them. My heart goes out to those who share these stories, my heart breaks for how they have been hurt and the ways they are suffering. I also believe that without restoration, we will often continue unhealthy patterns of responding out of our pain. There is a popular saying: "Hurt people, hurt people."[1] Essentially, if we have been hurt, we will in turn hurt others. I also believe the opposite is true:

> restored people will restore people.

As Christians, we are called to share fewer stories and more testimonies: testimonies of those who have walked the hard road of the Paschal Mystery and are now walking in the freedom that only Jesus can bring; testimonies of how we were lost and have been found, were blind and now we see. As Christian disciples, we are all called to mission, to be heralds of the miracles God has done in our lives. The glorified body of Jesus shows us that as we experience resurrection, our scars are to become signs of glory and a testimony for others. As we are restored, we are invited to share in the mission of Christ to proclaim freedom and liberty to those who are still held captive. Twenty-three years ago, I read a passage from Isaiah that speaks directly to this and has become a life scripture for me:

> The spirit of the Lord GOD is upon me,
>   because the LORD has anointed me;
> he has sent me to bring good news to the oppressed,
>   to bind up the brokenhearted,
> to proclaim liberty to the captives,
>   and release to the prisoners;
> to proclaim the year of the LORD's favor,
>   and the day of vengeance of our God;
>   to comfort all who mourn;
> to provide for those who mourn in Zion—
>   to give them a garland instead of ashes,
> the oil of gladness instead of mourning,
>   the mantle of praise instead of a faint spirit.
> They will be called oaks of righteousness,
>   the planting of the LORD, to display his glory. (Is 61:1–3)

Becoming heralds of the miracles God has done is the call for all of us who are baptized Christians. To do that we must have a personal encounter with Jesus and share from the perspective of an eyewitness just as the apostles did.

> That which was from the beginning, which we have heard, which we have seen with our eyes, which we have looked at and our hands have touched, this we proclaim concerning the Word of life—this life was revealed, and we have seen it and testify to it, and declare to you the eternal life that was with the Father and was revealed to us—we declare to you what we have seen and heard so that you also may have fellowship with us; and truly our fellowship is with the Father and with his Son Jesus Christ. (1 Jn 1:1–3)

It's not enough for people to hear about a God we *know* about; they need to hear about a God we have *encountered*, have been loved by, have been healed by, and who wants to do the same in their lives.

I believe that in the unique and specific places we have experienced healing, we are called to be a channel of God's healing in the same areas for others.

We often like to rush to be the helper or the healer before we have been helped and healed ourselves. This doesn't mean we have to be perfectly healed before we can share with others, but we do have to be engaged in the Paschal Mystery and experiencing real movement in our personal relationship with Jesus. We all know far too many people, priests, religious, and laypeople who are in roles in ministry but have not addressed their own wounds. Often these are the people and places in the Church where we have experienced a lot of pain, and the Church has experienced a significant amount of scandal. All of us need to repent and experience metanoia, a conversion of heart, if we want to see the restoration power of God at work, and *it begins with you and me.* "If my people who are called by my name humble themselves, pray, seek my face, and turn from their wicked ways, then I will hear from heaven, and will forgive their sin and heal their land" (2 Chr 7:14).

Our God is a God of miracles; he is a healer and a restorer. Each of us has places within us that need our God to be who he is and bring the dead places to life, but we need to ask. We are invited to give up our own way and surrender to his will, his way, and experience the full life he has in store. As we experience that, people will see God at work and desire to experience this freedom also.

We don't need a platform to share our testimonies we just need to open the door in the relationships that God has placed before us, invite the Holy Spirit to come, and let him do the rest.

Pause & REFLECT

Take some time to journal and reflect on the following questions:

What are some signs of glory, places where you have personally experienced Christ and his love, in your life?

Who in your life is Christ calling you to share your story with?

Who might Christ be calling you to disciple?

CONCLUSION

You and I are made for more. The pain, despair, brokenness, lies, and mediocrity we are experiencing in parts of our life right now is not how it is meant to be or how it needs to continue to be. Life to the fullest is possible. It is why Jesus came. "I have come that they may have life, and have it to the full" (Jn 10:10 NIV). We have an invitation from Jesus to not settle for a life in bondage but live in the freedom he designed us for. We are made to be free and to deeply abide in the love of God,

---

and we do not have to wait until heaven
to start experiencing it.

The thing about the journey is that it's not fast. We all wish we could skip some steps or fast-forward parts of it, but we can't. We must be willing to travel through the whole thing. The journey to freedom, healing, wholeness, and abiding is a lifetime process, but thankfully we get to experience measures of it along the way. If I've learned anything from my own years of journeying into self-awareness and healing, it is that

---

the journey is where Jesus is.

He's not waiting at the end as the prize for a job well done. He is with us, every step of the way. He says to us in scripture, "Be strong and courageous. Do not be afraid; do not be discouraged, for the Lord your God will be with you wherever you go" (Jos 1:9 NIV).

As we encounter all of the parts of our story, as we uncover our wounds, we will find ourselves in places of utter poverty and littleness, but we will also find Jesus there, in his fullness. The smaller and more vulnerable we get, the more space there is for his beauty, truth, and goodness to enter into our lives. He is with us, he is good, and he will never leave us.

I encourage you to never let fear or hopelessness get in the way of the full life Jesus has for you. It's not as much about what we can do but about what he can do in us. If you feel this is too much for you, too hard for you, and too painful for you, it's okay. You're not wrong; it is too much for us, but it's not too much for Jesus our Savior. These are the places we desperately need the Savior to save us so we don't have to carry the weight of it anymore. Jesus wants to carry our burdens. I love the scripture from 2 Corinthians 12:9–11 when Paul says, "But he said to me, 'My grace is sufficient for you, for my power is made perfect in weakness.' Therefore I will boast all the more gladly about my weaknesses, so that Christ's power may rest on me. That is why, for Christ's sake, I delight in weaknesses, in insults, in hardships, in persecutions, in difficulties. For when I am weak, then I am strong."

The scriptures I'm speaking here aren't trite or shallow comments; they are the truth God has spoken to us. They are anchors for us that give us hope in the promises of God. My prayer is that you would cling to these promises and be willing to enter into the journey. I hope that this book goes beyond some good ideas or suggestions and moves you further in the healing journey and closer to Jesus. I invite you to pray with me:

Jesus, I open my heart to you. I offer you all of my fears, doubts, and wounds and ask that you would come and be with me in my deepest need. I need you, Jesus. I need your love and your presence to teach me about who I am and who you have called me to be. I ask that you would let your light shine into the dark places of my heart and my memories. Help me to see where you are and reveal to me the things you desire to heal and restore. I open my heart and surrender to the power of your resurrection in my life. Please guide me into greater freedom and wholeness and may I always know you are with me. Amen.

ACKNOWLEDGMENTS

I would first like to thank my family for their continual love and all the ways they support me and the ministry that has been entrusted to me. You're my favorites. To Michelle Benzinger and Sr. Miriam James Heidland, thank you for your friendship through the ups and downs, the joys and sorrows. Thank you for allowing me to be little, for being willing to speak the truth, and inspiring me to go deeper. I'm grateful for all the intercessors in my life, especially Mary Kyne, who has been a steady companion and prophetic voice along the journey of life. I'm grateful for my dear friend and spiritual director, Fr. Justin Brady, who has battled for my freedom and has always helped me remember my story and the calling God has for my life. My deepest thanks to Fr. Dave Pivonka, TOR, for writing the foreword for this book, but more importantly, I'm thankful for him as a kindred spirit, a father in his priesthood, and a big brother at pivotal moments in my life. His witness of faith and abandonment to the will of God has been a source of inspiration for me to give my all to Jesus and for his kingdom. I'd like to thank my favorite catechetics professor at Franciscan University, Sr. M. Johanna Paruch, FSGM, who taught me about the power of scripture and the responsibility of being a teacher of the faith. I'm so grateful for the circle of powerful, holy, and Spirit-filled women in ministry, The Committed, whom I have had the privilege of sitting at their feet and linking arms with. I would like to thank my local community of friends, the Home Builder families, Brett and Andrea Powell, and Archbishop J. Michael Miller, CSB, shepherd of the Archdiocese of Vancouver, for all of your support and encouragement. Many thanks to Kristi McDonald, Catherine Owers, and the Ave Maria Press team for all of your hard work and help to make this book a reality. Finally, I would like to thank Jesus, my dearest friend, my steady shelter, my savior, and the lover of my soul. You are my everything.

NOTES

2. We Have a Story

1. Gus Van Sant, dir., *Good Will Hunting* (Miramax, 1997).

2. John Paul II, "17th World Youth Day: Homily," July 28, 2002, https://www.vatican.va/content/john-paul-ii/en./homilies/2002/documents/hf_jp-ii_hom_20020728_xvii-wyd.html

3. John Paul II, "15th World Youth Day: Vigil of Prayer (*Tor Vergata*)," August 19, 2000, www.vatican.va/content/john-paul-ii/en/speeches/2000/jul-sep/documents/hf_jp-ii_spe_20000819_gmg-veglia.html.

3. We Have an Enemy

1. Teresa of Avila, *The Interior Castle* (San Bernardino, CA: Createspace Independent Publishing, 2017), "First Mansions," chapter 1.

4. Blocks to Healing

1. "Forgiveness: Your Health Depends on It," Johns Hopkins Medicine, 2019, http://www.hopkinsmedicine.org/health/wellness-and-prevention/forgiveness-your-health-depends-on-it.

2. Alex Witchel, "At Lunch With: Malachy McCourt—How a Rogue Turns Himself into a Saint; the Blarney Fails to Hide an Emotional Directness," *New York Times*, July 29, 1998, http://www.nytimes.com/1998/07/29/books/lunch-with-malachy-mccourt-rogue-turns-himself-into-saint-blarney-fails-hide.html. Accessed 11 Aug. 2021.

3. J. R. R. Tolkien, *The Return of the King: Being the Third Part of the Lord of the Rings* (New York: Ballantine Books, 2012).

4. Peter Jackson, dir., *The Lord of the Rings: The Two Towers* (New Line Home Entertainment; distributed by Alliance Films, 2011).

5. Francis Lawrence, dir., *Hunger Games: Mockingjay, Part 2* (Lionsgate, 2015).

5. The Personality of Jesus
1. Dallas Jenkins, dir., *The Chosen* (Loaves & Fishes Productions, Angel Studios, 2017).

6. Jesus the Way
1. John Paul II, "Apostolic Journey to the United States of America: Eucharistic Celebration in Oriole Park at Camden Yards, Baltimore (8 October 1995) | John Paul II," *www.vatican.va*, 8 Oct. 1995, www.vatican.va/content/john-paul-ii/en/homilies/1995/documents/hf_jp-ii_hom_19951008_baltimore.html.

2. Fulton J. Sheen, *Life of Christ* (1977; Toronto: Random House Canada, 2008), 63, Kindle.

7. Jesus the Truth
1. John Paul II, "General Audience: Man Enters the World as a Subject of Truth and Love," February 20, 1980. www.vatican.va/content/john-paul-ii/en/audiences/1980/documents/hf_jp-ii_aud_19800220.html

2. Joe Wright, dir., *Pride & Prejudice* (Universal Pictures, 2005).

3. Augustine of Hippo. *The Confessions of Saint Augustine* (Mount Vernon, NY: Peter Pauper Press, 1949), book 10, chapter 27 (38).

8. Jesus the Life
1. Benedict XVI, "45th World Day of Peace 2012: Educating Young People in Justice and Peace," January 20, 2012, www.vatican.va/content/benedict-xvi/en/messages/peace/documents/hf_ben-xvi_mes_20111208_xlv-world-day-peace.html.

2. John Paul II, "Pastoral Visit to Poland, 46th International Eucharistic Congress," June 1, 1997, https://www.vatican.va/content/john-paul-ii/en/travels/1997/documents/hf_jp-ii_spe_01061997_statio-orbis.html.

9. Essentials in the Journey of Healing
1. C. S. Lewis, *The Voyage of the Dawn Treader* (1952; New York: HarperCollins, 1994).

10. Signs of Glory

1. Charles Eads, "The Polk Street Professor," Amarillo (TX) Globe-Times, February 26, 1959, 30.

Heather Khym is the cohost of the internationally popular *Abiding Together* podcast. She and her husband, Jake, are the cofounders of Life Restoration Ministries, where she serves as director of vision and ministry of the British Columbia–based apostolate. She also serves as director of the Celtic Cross Foundation.

Khym has more than twenty-five years of experience as a speaker and retreat leader who offers workshops and conferences in the United States and Canada. She attended Franciscan University of Steubenville, studying theology and catechetics.

Khym is passionate about evangelization, discipleship, and creating an environment that leads people to a personal encounter with God. She works with and volunteers in a number of capacities for the Archdiocese of Vancouver and served on the archbishop's pastoral council for six years.

She lives with her husband and three children in British Columbia, Canada.

liferestoration.ca/

abidingtogetherpodcast.com

Twitter: @abidingpodcast

Instagram: @heatherkhym

YouTube: Abiding Together Podcast

Fr. Dave Pivonka, TOR, is the president of Franciscan University of Steubenville.